Duet or Duel?

Duet or Duel?

Theology and Science
in a Postmodern World

J. Wentzel van Huyssteen

The 1998 Diocese of British Columbia
John Albert Hall Lectures
at the
Centre for Studies in Religion and Society
in the University of Victoria

TRINITY PRESS INTERNATIONAL
HARRISBURG, PENNSYLVANIA

Copyright © J. Wentzel van Huyssteen 1998

Library of Congress Cataloging-in-Publication Data

Van Huyssteen, Wentzel.
  Duet or duel? : theology and science in a postmodern world / J.
Wentzel van Huyssteen.
     p. cm.
  "The 1998 Diocese of British Columbia John Albert Hall
lectures at the Centre for Studies in Religion and Society in the
University of Victoria."
  Includes bibliographical references and index.
  ISBN 1-56338-255-5 (pbk. : alk. paper)
  1. Religion and science. 2. Knowledge, Theory of (Religion)
3. Human evolution—Religious aspects. 4. Postmodernism—
Religious aspects. I. Title.
BL241.V35   1998
261.5'5—dc21   98-33514
                                                          CIP

First North American Edition 1998
by Trinity Press International
P.O. Box 1321
Harrisburg, PA 17105

Trinity Press International is part
of the Morehouse Group.
Printed in Great Britain

THE JOHN ALBERT HALL LECTURES

Churchman, chemist, pioneer, soldier, businessman and philanthropist, John Albert Hall (1869–1933) emigrated from Britain to Canada in the last decade of the nineteenth century and made his home in Victoria, British Columbia. He left a legacy to the Diocese of British Columbia to found a lectureship to stimulate harmony between the Christian religion and contemporary thought. Colonel Hall's generosity sustained the work of three successive Canon Lecturers: Michael Coleman, Hilary Butler and Thomas Bailey. It also helped found the Greater Victoria Lay School of Theology. Since 1995 it has been supporting the lectureship's partnership between the Diocese of British Columbia and the University of Victoria's Centre for Studies in Religion and Society.

The Centre was established in 1991 to foster the scholarly study of religion in relation to the sciences, ethics, social and economic development, and other aspects of culture. As Co-sponsor of the John Albert Hall Lecture Series it assists in the fulfilment of the terms of the trust.

John Albert Hall lecturers are outstanding Christian theologians who address themselves to the church, the university and the community during a two-week Fellowship in Victoria, Canada. Publication of these lectures allows a wider audience to benefit from both the lecture series and the work of the Centre.

Contents

Acknowledgments

This book contains the John Albert Hall Lectures which I gave at the University of Victoria in British Columbia, Canada, in January 1998. I am very grateful to the Anglican Synod of the Diocese of British Columbia, and to the Centre for Studies in Religion and Society at the University of Victoria, for the gracious invitation to give these lectures. My wife, Hester, and I were made to feel completely at home in Victoria, and we deeply appreciate the tremendous hospitality and the kindness of our hosts there.

The invitation to give the John Albert Hall Lectures at the University of Victoria also gave me the opportunity to incorporate some of the materials I have recently been working on, and lecturing in, at Princeton Theological Seminary. I owe so much to the wonderfully challenging and outstanding students at Princeton Seminary. I am also deeply grateful to my own institution for creating a truly exceptional, stimulating, and rewarding atmosphere to pursue my own interests in interdisciplinary theology.

The groundwork for these lectures was laid when BBC North invited me to be part of a televised Religion and Science special, filmed by their Religious Programmes Department in Brno, the Czech Republic, during September 1996. I am especially indebted to Anna Laura Malago and Anne

Duet or Duel?

Greevell, producers of BBC TV's *Heart of the Matter*, for including me in this unique event. I greatly enjoyed working with, and getting to know, Richard Dawkins, Baroness Mary Warnock, Michael Heller and David Starkey.

I am deeply indebted to my wife, Hester, for her wonderful and enduring support and for being willing to sacrifice most of our Christmas 1997 holidays to enable me to finish these lectures. A very special word of thanks goes to my research assistant, David M. Carlson, for all his support and for his excellent work in editing the text and creating the index. I also remember, with much appreciation, Professor Stefan Veldsman, who already in 1987 suggested the title 'Duet or Duel?' for my very first public lecture in Theology and Science at the University of Port Elizabeth, South Africa.

J. Wentzel van Huyssteen
Princeton Theological Seminary
Winter 1997/1998

Preface

In these lectures I will focus on the special place of theology in the current interdisciplinary conversation. Within the wider domain of interdisciplinary reflection, the ongoing theology and science dialogue seems to be alive and well as more and more theologians, and scientists who are also theologians, are publishing on an increasingly wider range of topics. Already the mere pursuit of interdisciplinary reflection, however, is turning out to be one of the most challenging intellectual quests today as rigid, modernist, disciplinary distinctions seem to be breaking down and new spaces open up for cross-disciplinary conversation.

The idea of finding a plausible model for interdisciplinary reflection seems all the more amazing when we take seriously at least some of the pluralism and fragmentation normally associated with postmodern thought. Even the briefest overview of the contemporary North American theological scene already reveals the startling fragmentation and pluralism arising from the kind of radical critique we now are calling the 'postmodern challenge'. In any radical fragmentation of our knowledge, the dialogue between theology and science would be one of the first casualties. I hope to show, however, that although the problem of pluralism in theology and science directly relates to the rather dramatic emergence of so-called contextual or 'local' modes of reflection, there are also positive and constructive ways in which we could take this kind of postmodernism seriously. This will be achieved by not giving up too easily our quest for the kind of comprehensive epistemology that would yield true interdisciplinary reflection.

One of the important goals of this book will be to argue that for theology this complex situation presents a confusing double challenge. Theological reflection now certainly seems to be firmly enveloped in postmodernism's radical pluralism. However, it often also – and paradoxically – still seems to be caught up in the kind of modernist dilemma where an allegedly superior scientific rationality is invariably opposed to religious faith as a privatized form of subjective experience and opinion. This leaves theology also still firmly embedded in the stark, modernist separation between knowledge and opinion, explanation and understanding, natural and human sciences, and epistemology and hermeneutics. In this confusing context theological reflection can only suffer complete intellectual marginalization. Both postmodernism's epistemic pluralism and modernism's marginalization of religious meaning have therefore been very successful in deconstructing our attempts to find possible shared resources of human rationality from which all our reasoning strategies – also disciplines as diverse as theology and the sciences – may benefit in cross-disciplinary reflection.

In this book I will therefore specifically address the issue of theology's epistemic isolation in a pluralistic world and then directly argue for the interdisciplinary nature and status of theological reflection. The dilemma for the philosophical theologian is, of course, that both the historicist deconstruction of Western metaphysics and the aftermath of the collapse of all epistemological foundationalism have not only rendered the feasibility of any attempt at a comprehensive approach to human knowledge and rationality impossible, but have revealed the very possibility of public, interdisciplinary discourse as profoundly problematical.

To counter this argument, I will argue that precisely in the interdisciplinary conversation between theology and the sciences of cosmology and evolutionary biology there are rich resources for retrieving a comprehensive approach to human knowledge that would be neither modernist nor foundationalist. As we will see, much of contemporary cosmology argues for treating the observable universe as a single object, and therefore implies that the universe has intelligibility as a single object of study. This will also imply, however, a comprehensive epistemology that reflects the interdisciplinary nature of this mode of knowledge. In this sense contemporary cosmology may offer a positive response to the postmodern disillusionment with all totalizing forms of knowledge and may succeed in pointing the way to a comprehensive epistemology that might actually still enhance and elucidate our interdisciplinary reflection without subsuming it under the dominance of ideological metanarratives.

I will also argue that theological reflection is radically shaped not only by its social, historical and cultural context, but also by the biological roots of human rationality. Especially in contemporary evolutionary epistemology we will find surprising, if not startling, attempts to facilitate precisely the challenge of a constructive form of postmodernism: the need for a more comprehensive and integrated approach to the problem of human knowledge. Evolutionary epistemology, rightly understood, reveals the biological roots of all human rationality and should therefore lead precisely to an interdisciplinary account of our epistemic activities. The basic assumption of evolutionary epistemology is that we humans, like all other living beings, result from evolutionary processes and that, consequently, our mental capacities are constrained and shaped by the mechanisms of biological evolution. I will accept, at least in a minimalist sense, that all our knowledge, including our scientific and religious knowledge, is grounded in biological evolution. And if human knowledge results from, and is shaped by, evolution, then the study of evolution will be of extreme importance for an understanding of the phenomenon of knowledge.

I will also show why evolutionary epistemology meets the need for facilitating a postfoundationalist notion of rationality that takes us beyond traditional disciplinary boundaries. Evolutionary epistemology, rightly understood, will therefore facilitate an interdisciplinary account of all our epistemic activities. Thus I will argue that Darwin (and neo-Darwinism) was right in arguing that metaphysical and religious beliefs in humans are related to evolutionary processes and that human rationality therefore has strong biological roots. I will also argue, however, that although this may explain away deistic notions of God, it does not fully explain religious belief, and certainly not belief in God as such.

An exploration into the interdisciplinary nature of theological reflection should therefore not only facilitate the revisioning of the nature and standards of theological reflection, but should also show how firmly religion and religious reflection are embedded in our culture today. Probing the problem of interdisciplinary reflection in a postfoundationalist mode should therefore lead to the growing awareness that human rationality can never be adequately housed within one specific reasoning strategy only. To recognize that religious reflection shares in the rich resources of human rationality is to open our eyes to the fact that this rationality itself is operative between our different modes of knowledge and therefore links together different disciplines and reasoning strategies. The mere awareness of this fact, of course, already reveals the breakdown of the traditional modernist demarcation between science and religion/theology.

In Chapter One I will briefly explore the thesis that postmodernism, as a contemporary cultural phenomenon, has been unable to come to terms with the issue of human rationality in any positive way. As a result of this, many of the stereotyped ways of relating theology and science through models of conflict, independence, consonance, harmony, or dialogue will be revealed as overly simplistic generalizations about the complex relationship between these two dominant forces in our culture. Postmodern pluralism makes it very difficult even to speak so generally about 'rationality', 'science', 'religion', 'theology', 'God', or 'divine action' today. The postmodern mood in theology and science, however, also challenges the special and superior status of the natural sciences and thus will open up new avenues for dialogue between these radically different disciplines.

In Chapter Two we will see how difficult it is to imagine a universe less staggering, dramatic, and mysterious, for all its rationality and intelligibility, than our universe. Even more fascinating, however, will be the fact that contemporary cosmology argues for treating the observable universe as a single object, which therefore implies that the universe must somehow have intelligibility as a single object of study. In conversation with the very different views of Stephen Hawking and Paul Davies, we will trace what it might mean that we human beings seem to carry the spark of rationality that provides the key to understanding our universe. Exactly this point will be our cue as we proceed to search for the kind of comprehensive epistemology that might yield the interdisciplinary nature of this mode of knowledge. And it is here that we will see that contemporary cosmology may actually offer a positive response to the postmodern disillusionment with all totalizing forms of knowledge. This will be found in the fact that theology and cosmology, although widely diverse as reasoning strategies, are both essentially interdisciplinary in nature and as such share deeply in the quest for a more comprehensive and interrelated knowledge of the origin, meaning and destiny of our universe. This almost necessarily presupposes and implies a kind of comprehensive epistemology that would reflect precisely the interdisciplinary nature of this mode of knowledge.

In Chapter Three we will focus on the fact that biology and theology are obviously based on modes of knowledge, reasoning strategies and methodologies that are radically different. They do, however, share one focal interest, i.e., an interest in what we may call life processes: obviously, the discovery of fundamental life processes and their structure and manifestations is the explicit task of biology. Exactly these life processes, at least in a broader sense, fall under the interdisciplinary scope of theology too, because the Judeo-Christian belief in creation traditionally brings into focus the origin of life itself. To highlight the enduring nature of this problem, we will engage with Charles Darwin, and with the response of one of Darwin's most important North American contemporaries to the theory of evolution by natural selection. As theology's ongoing interdisciplinary conversation with philosophy and cosmology will show, theological reflection is deeply concerned with some of life's most profound and ultimate questions. Exactly for these reasons the theological world view by definition implies a radical reinterpretation of the world from an informed Christian point of view. I will then argue, against Richard Dawkins, that a theological redescription of the process of evolution and a creative complementary integration of the results of contemporary evolutionary biology could indeed be eminently rational and could offer a persuasive alternative to resolutely scientistic or radically naturalistic readings of the same material. I also believe, along with some other Christian theologians, that a responsible theological redescription of these issues should make it clear why the idea of God, and of God's presence in this universe, can move us beyond disputes like whether evolution operates through blind chance or providence, whether naturalism or supernaturalism are the only options open to Christian believers, and whether we should, therefore, feel forced to choose between these two narrow options as the only available constructs for explaining the origin and evolution of life on our planet. I therefore believe that evolution, rightly understood, can enrich our religious faith considerably, and may actually set the stage for a friendly and rewarding 'duet' between religion and science.

Finally, in Chapter Four, we will look at the evolutionary fact that, with human consciousness and culture, radically new elements like conscious experiences have come into existence, and, as we will see, along with thoughts have also come values, purposes, and ultimately a propensity for rational knowledge. It is precisely in an attempt to understand our own ability to cope intelligently with an increasingly intelligible world through knowledge that the impact of the theory of evolution is felt far beyond the boundaries of biology. Because of this I will especially focus on the important discipline of evolutionary epistemology. My claim will be that evolutionary epistemology not only yields the kind of postfoundationalist, comprehensive epistemology that has eluded us in a sceptical postmodernist context, but might actually help us to rediscover the resources of human rationality that I believe are shared so deeply by both theology and the sciences. In contemporary evolutionary epistemology, then, we will find surprising and exciting attempts to facilitate precisely the challenge of a constructive form of postmodernism: the need for a more comprehensive and integrated approach to the problem of human knowledge.

By revealing the biological origins of all human rationality, evolutionary epistemology could possibly point the way to precisely the safe kind of epistemological space we require for a graceful interdisciplinary duet between theology and the sciences. As theologians we should be able to enter this pluralist, cross-disciplinary conversation with our personal religious convictions intact and at the same time be theoretically empowered to step beyond the limitations and boundaries of our own religious and disciplinary contexts. This epistemological option for theological reflection is a plausible option because, despite widely divergent personal, disciplinary, or religious viewpoints, we still share – even in a pluralist, postmodern culture – the rich resources of human rationality.

I

A Safe Space for Theology and Science?

Interdisciplinary Reflection beyond the Postmodern Challenge

The challenges facing those of us who cautiously enter the complex and multifaceted dialogue between theology and the sciences today are often daunting, if not confusing. The enduring successes and prestige of the natural sciences, as well as their ubiquitous presence all over the world today, still serve to ensure the almost universal aura of science and the myth of the superiority of natural scientific rationality. In glaring contrast to this image of science, religion – and certainly the Christian faith – has never been just a set of intellectual beliefs, or a universally accepted set of theoretical ideas and experimental results, but has always first of all involved a way of life for very specific communities of faith. Religious communities are typically exemplified by distinctive forms of individual experience, communal rituals and specific ethical concerns (cf. Barbour 1990: xiii), and – most importantly – by a very specific focus on the transformation of personal life. This religious quest for personal transformation, for the Christian at least, has always also been deeply embedded in the powerful truth claims of this faith, and in

I

the fact that for the Christian, the story of God's creation and salvation, and especially of God's action in the world, has always provided a cosmic setting in which individual lives have found their own significance.

In the long and troubled history of the relation between theology and science, this has more often than not led to conflicting truth claims between these two very different reasoning strategies. More recently the dialogue between theology and the sciences has been forced into a rather radical conflict, a kind of modernist 'duel' where 'objective', universal scientific claims were starkly contrasted to conflict with subjective, 'irrational' theological beliefs, resulting in a relentless pressure toward the absolute polarization of religion and science (cf. Bell 1996: 179). For those of us who are theologians, and who are trying to move beyond this popular and ubiquitous conflict-image in an attempt to find a safe epistemological space for the dialogue between theology and the sciences, the interdisciplinary nature of this discussion forms a very specific challenge: a challenge to reflect once again on the nature and task of theological reflection and on the values that shape theological and scientific reflection. This is especially important since, in our century, we human beings have come to know who we are and where we are in ways unprecedented in all past millennia. We know the size, age, and extent of our universe, and we know the deep evolutionary history of our planet and ourselves as part of this magnificent story (cf. Rolston 1996: 61).

As we will soon see, contemporary culture, with all its amazing diversity, is confronting us with yet another disconcerting challenge, that of an alleged postmodern attitude. Postmodernity challenges us to deal with the fact that we have clearly been robbed of any general, universal, or abstract ways to talk about the relationship between religion and science today. The only way in which this complex but important relationship can really be adequately approached would be by looking at how it plays out contextually. This is also the reason why Ian Barbour's well-known, and helpful, fourfold taxonomy for relating religion and science through either conflict, dialogue, independence or integration (cf. Barbour 1990: 3–30) may now be too generic, too universal, as categories that intend to catch the complexity of the ongoing exchange between these two dominant forces in our culture. Holmes Rolston is right, therefore, when he claims a much more nuanced approach: at present, for example, there may be more dialogue and integration between physics, cosmology and theology; but between biology and theology there certainly is ample conflict and considerable independence (cf. 1996: 61f.). For Rolston, the question whether, and how, this trend will continue depends on discoveries as yet unknown in physics, astronomy, and in molecular and evolutionary biology.

Niels Henrik Gregersen and I have recently argued, however, that this problem may be even more complex, and that the contextual pluralism so typical of postmodernism has virtually exploded the neat distinction between these four well-known and influential categories (cf. Gregersen and J. W. van Huyssteen 1998: 1ff.). To cope adequately with this complex, interdisciplinary relationship we may now have to descend to an even deeper level and ask what it is about the human mind, and its ability to construct different forms of human knowledge, that has enabled us even to develop the seemingly radically diverse reasoning strategies of theology and science. Another way of putting this question would be as follows: what are the origins and roots of human rationality, and how did this lead to science and religion, arguably the two most dominant forces in human culture today?

I will argue in these lectures that, while the rationality of theological reflection is shaped by its concrete embeddedness in specific traditions, it also is definitively shaped by its location in the living context of interdisciplinary reflection. I will also argue that the ability to have this kind of interdisciplinary conversation is possible only because human rationality as such has deep and significant biological origins. Furthermore, this kind of interdisciplinary context is – epistemologically at least – significantly shaped by the dominant presence and influence of scientific rationality in our culture. To explore the ramifications of this for the dialogue between theology and science, however, we will first have to affirm the respective epistemological integrities of both theology and the sciences as very different modes of reflection. More importantly, we will have to explore what it means for this particular dialogue to be a subset of the much larger problem of interdisciplinary reflection.

A new pluralism in theology

Trying to find some kind of meaningful epistemological link between theology and science not only confronts us with the problem of interdisciplinary reflection as we attempt to bring together two modes of knowledge as diverse as theology and science, but also presents us with another acute new problem: even the briefest overview of the contemporary North American theological scene reveals the startling fragmentation effected by what is often called the 'postmodern challenge'. The radical pluralization of sceptical forms of postmodernism has not only directly influenced theology, but is also – as we will see – shaping our reflections about science and philosophy of science. Much of postmodernist thought has also turned out to be a deconstruction of any of our attempts to identify the shared resources of human rationality from which all disciplines – even those as diverse as theology and science – may have benefitted in cross-disciplinary reflection. Furthermore, we have by now also learned to be more careful in our attempts to understand the elusive phenomenon of postmodernism: postmodernism is not just a new cultural phase after modernity, nor just a new 'period' in cultural history, and it certainly is not just a new set of beliefs, a theory, or a doctrine. Postmodernism is, rather, an attitude, a radically different way of looking at the world of modernity, a mood that has also slowly and pervasively filtered into the way we think, and especially now into the way we do theology and science too. Unfortunately, many scientists and theologians have also wrongly learned to associate postmodernism only with a rampant pluralism, with a jettisoning of reason and of epistemology, and with some form of sceptical, gloomy and negative deconstructionism.

The dilemma for the theologian interested in interdisciplinary conversation with the natural sciences is of course that the postmodern deconstruction of Western metaphysics and epistemological foundationalism has now rendered the very possibility of a public or cross-disciplinary conversation extremely problematical. Theology at the end of the twentieth century is certainly marked by an inescapable pluralism which not only threatens traditional academic theology, but makes interdisciplinary dialogue almost impossible. Instead of 'one true theology', the discarding of modernity's meta-narratives has now led both to the recognition of the import-

ance of discrete experiences and specific traditions in theological reflection, and to the inevitable emergence of so-called
'local theologies' (cf. Byrne 1994: 6). These theologies are not
only local in the sense of ethnic or cultural theologies, but
also 'local' in the specific sense of radically contextual theologies growing from particular experiences (e.g. liberation
theologies, womanist and feminist theologies, eco-theologies,
gay and lesbian theologies, and various forms of evangelical
or post-liberal theologies which also claim to be forms of
postmodern theology). The way in which these diverse forms
of theological reflection involve a serious and conscious
choice for very specific traditions, or even neglected aspects of
the Christian tradition, shows not only that tradition and
local context always go together closely, but also that contemporary theological pluralism has almost rendered it meaningless to talk about the 'theology' side of 'theology and
science' as if the existence of one true theology could still be
posited in such a generic, uncomplicated way.

Any overview of the contemporary theological landscape
in our culture will quickly reveal how startling the fragmentation is, caused by 'the postmodern challenge' of our
times. The radical pluralization following sceptical forms of
postmodern critique has, however, not only affected different
theologies in different ways, but also seriously undermined
attempts to construct a safe epistemological space where, as
theologians, we might be taken seriously in interdisciplinary
dialogue. For the Christian theologian this has serious implications, and questions like the following haunt some of us all
the time. In a radically pluralist world where epistemological
foundationalism has been so successfully deconstructed, will
it still be possible for theology to join other modes of knowledge in some form of interdisciplinary, public discourse? Or

is the only coherent and consistent way to defend theological truth-claims to fall back massively on our respective traditions and to hope that some form of local consensus will emerge there and pave the way to whatever we see as the 'truth'?

As theologians, we have hopefully now learned to avoid the arrogance of prescribing overarching, foundationalist rules for interdisciplinary dialogue. But we should just as seriously avoid the insular comfort of nonfoundationalist isolationism, where instead of seeing our preferred tradition(s) as our only access to interdisciplinary dialogue, we retreat to isolated and sectarian forms of theological rationality that would preclude the possibility of a meaningful dialogue with the sciences. In these lectures I will therefore argue that in order to talk meaningfully about God, and about God's action in the world, we require a safe space where theology and science – instead of being in endless conflict – can engage in the 'graceful duet' of true interdisciplinary reflection. This presupposes that we reflect about the problem of human rationality, about the biological origins of this rationality, and about the values that shape the rationality of both theological and scientific reflection. I want to argue that, as far as theology goes, this quest for the nature and origins of human rationality – which will have implications for how good theology ought to be done – should be approached in terms of the following strong claims:

First, we relate to our world through interpreted experience. As such we have no standing ground, no place for evaluating, judging and enquiring, apart from that which is provided by the context of some specific tradition(s) (cf. MacIntyre 1988: 350). From a constructive, positive postmodern awareness, we have already learned that 'theology and science' will only make sense if the 'theology' part of this dialogue is firmly rooted in the context of (a) very specific tradition(s).

Second, because we cannot think and act except through an engagement with tradition, our task is to stand in a critical relation to our tradition, and thereby 'split the difference' between modernity and postmodernity (cf. Schrag 1992: 166), aiming to capture those features of science which indeed make it a paradigmatically rational enterprise without, however, falling back on universalizing, modernist views of human rationality. This implies a step beyond the confines of particular traditions and will be warranted by a revised and postfoundationalist notion of rationality where the task and identity of theology is definitively shaped by its location in the living context of interdisciplinary reflection.

Third, this contemporary interdisciplinary context is – epistemologically, at least – significantly shaped by the dominant presence and the ubiquity of scientific rationality in our culture. Often focusing on the unique hermeneutics of theological reflection, theologians have notoriously neglected this profound epistemological challenge by ignoring, or not recognizing, the pervasive influence of the sciences on the epistemic and other values that shape theological rationality.

During the course of these lectures we will see how these claims play out in two of the most celebrated areas for conflicts and duels between theology and science, i.e., contemporary cosmology and evolutionary biology. Strong claims for the intellectual superiority of these influential sciences often lead to equally urgent pleas for the autonomy and unique nature of religious faith and religious experience. This, of course, will always fuel conflicts in the ongoing

8

debate between theology and science. Unfortunately, however, it also reinforces some confusing stereotypes that have kept alive some of the typical or 'classical' problems of this debate. The most important of these problems reveal strong contradictions (cf. Theissen 1984: 4ff.) between scientific thought and religious faith and are normally stated as follows (cf. J. W. van Huyssteen 1997a: 239f.):

- scientific statements are hypothetical, fallible and tentative, while statements of religious faith are dogmatic, ideological and fideistic;
- scientific thought is always open to critical evaluation, justification or falsification, while religious faith goes against the facts and often defies empirical evidence;
- scientific thought delights in critical dissent and constructive criticism, while faith more often than not depends on massive consensus and uncritical commitment;
- scientists therefore seem to base their beliefs on evidence and rational argument, while religious beliefs appear to be founded on 'faith' only;
- scientific rationality is thus revealed as not only a very manicured and disciplined form of human reflection, but as also incommensurable with, and vastly superior to, religious faith and theological reflection.

It comes as no surprise that, on this view, science emerges as the great alternative not only to religious faith (cf. Midgley 1992: 139), but especially to theology as a reflection on this faith. Many of us, in fact, did grow up learning an account of our intellectual history as the story of the steady triumph of science over superstition and ignorance (cf. Placher 1989: 14). Almost all of these stereotyped contrasts between science and religion, however, assume far too simple a picture of what both science and theology are about. When we dig deeper into this complex issue, therefore, much more will be revealed about the philosophical and epistemological prejudices which so often lead directly to locking theology and science into a confrontational 'duel'.

One of the primary goals of these lectures, therefore, will be to argue that, at least for theology, this complex situation presents a confusing double challenge. Theological reflection now certainly seems to be firmly enveloped in postmodernism's radical pluralism. However, it often also – and paradoxically – still seems to be caught up in the kind of modernist dilemma where an allegedly superior scientific rationality is invariably opposed to religious faith as a privatized form of subjective experience and opinion. This leaves theology also still firmly embedded in the stark, modernist separation between knowledge and opinion, explanation and understanding, natural and human sciences, epistemology and hermeneutics. In this confusing context theological reflection can only suffer complete intellectual marginalization. Both postmodernism's epistemic pluralism, and modernism's marginalization of religious meaning, have therefore been very successful in deconstructing our attempts to find possible shared resources of human rationality from which all our reasoning strategies – also disciplines as diverse as theology and the sciences – may benefit in cross-disciplinary reflection. For the theologian this has serious implications, and questions like the following have become an enduring challenge. In a radically pluralist and largely secular postmodern world, is it really possible for religious reflection to join the conversation of public discourse? Can and should theologians even try plausibly to defend the 'truth' of their knowledge claims in publicly coherent and consistent ways? Moreover, what would be the consequences for the self-understanding of the theologian and his/her theological task if theology should fail to become a credible voice in the complex interdisciplinary conversation? Not only theological reflection, though, but also contemporary science is firmly embedded in our contemporary culture and its complex challenges. Does science represent a coherent and consistent image today, and has it managed to escape some of the fragmentation that has been the fate of contemporary theology? It is to these questions that we must now turn.

Postmodernism in science?

Those of us who still may be thinking that an issue like 'Postmodernism in Theology and Science' sounds esoteric, if not downright cabalistic, obviously haven't been reading our newspapers lately. Recently, in ZYGON: The Journal of Religion and Science, I argued that postmodern science has certainly been making headlines all over North America (cf. J.W. van Huyssteen 1997b). As recently as 22 October 1996, The New York Times reported that Native American 'creationists', who reject the theory of evolution and other scientific explanations of human origins in favour of their own folklore, are fiercely resisting modern archeology. Prominent scholars who support the Native American cause predictably see science as the dominant religion of our times and as intruding where it has not been invited to determine human origins.[1] Not just tribal archeologists, however, but

---

[1] Cf. George Johnson, 'Indian Tribes' Creationists Thwart Archeologists', The New York Times, Tuesday, 22 October 1996, p.C13.

also Western archeologists who support the Native American cause are now publicly appealing to postmodernism as a way out of this tricky problem: not only are the limitations of scientific explanations highlighted, but science is seen as just one of many ways of knowing the world. The author of the *The New York Times* article goes a step further and actually labels this a kind of 'postmodern relativism' in which science is seen as just one more belief system.[2]

An even more celebrated case that really brought post-modern science to our doorsteps via the front page of *The New York Times*[3] occurred when Alan Sokal, the controversial New York University physicist, fed up with what he saw as the excesses of the academic left, tricked the social science journal *Social Text* into publishing a paper written as a parody on postmodern science as though it were a serious scholarly work.[4] In this paper Sokal gets his fifteen minutes of Warholian fame as he pretends to join the ranks of those postmodern scientists whom he typically, albeit naively, sees as epistemic relativists and anti-realists. In this hoax he pretends to show how apparent it has become that physical reality, no less than social reality, is at bottom a social and linguistic construct, and that scientific knowledge, far from ever being objective, reflects and encodes the dominant ideologies and power relations of the culture that produces it.[5] At the same time, however, Professor Sokal published another article in *Lingua Franca*: in this article he cheerfully

---

[2] Cf. ibid., p.C13.

[3] Cf. Janny Scott, 'Postmodern Gravity Deconstructed, Slyly', *The New York Times*, Saturday, 18 May 1996, p.A1, 22.

[4] Cf. Alan D. Sokal, 'Transgressing the Boundaries: Towards a Transformative Hermeneutics of Quantum Gravity', *Social Text* 46/47, Nos.1 and 2, Spring/Summer 1996, pp.217–52.

[5] Cf. Janny Scott, 'Postmodern Gravity Deconstructed, Slyly' (n. 3)

reveals that the *Social Text* article was written as a satirical hoax in which he wanted to expose the hollowness of post-modernism as it 'sacrifices' objectivity and reality.[6] This philosophically rather naive view of postmodern science was publicly and eerily echoed just a few weeks later when – again in *The New York Times* – John Horgan wrote that, like a mutant virus, postmodernism has infected not only philo-sophy and the social sciences, but even such alleged bastions of truth and objectivity as physics and chemistry. He goes on to label postmodern science 'ironic science' (ironic in the sense that science too has now been set free from the 'tyranny of truth' and is revealed to have multiple meanings, none of which are definite) and includes in this category con-temporary chaos theory, superstring theory and quantum theory, which unlike conventional science – which normally gives us 'truth' – allegedly functions to keep us in awe and to induce wonder for the many mysteries that conventional science has left unsolved.[7]

While some of us may want to salute the fact that post-modernism in science, along with the problem of interdisci-plinary dialogue, has now apparently made it in the media, it is still true that these popular versions of postmodernism remain fundamentally misguided and serve to confuse not only the issue of postmodernism in science, but especially what the postmodern challenge to the science and theology dialogue may entail. To understand, therefore, what a post-modern perspective might mean for the complex interdisci-plinary dialogue of which theology and science also neces-

---

[6] Cf. Alan Sokal, 'A Physicist Experiments with Cultural Studies', *Lingua Franca* 6, No.4, May/June 1996, pp.62–4.

[7] Cf. John Horgan, 'Science Set Free From Truth', *The New York Times,* 16 July 1996.

sarily form a part, we will have to move beyond these rather naive stereotypes of rampant relativism and the loss of all objectivity and reality. I will argue instead that a positive appropriation of constructive forms of postmodern critique in both theology and science will reveal the resources of rationality shared by these two seemingly very different reasoning strategies. In this way, too, a safe and truly post-foundationalist space for the interdisciplinary conversation between theology and the sciences will open up naturally.

Several theologians have recently analysed and commented on the ramifications of both constructive and deconstructive forms of postmodern critique for theological reflection (cf. Tilley 1995; Griffen, Beardslee and Holland 1989; Murphy and McClendon 1989). Despite the current flood of philo-sophical texts on postmodernism, relatively few attempts, however, have been made to measure the importance of postmodern ideas for science. Of course, Lyotard's influential *The Postmodern Condition* (1984) focussed on science and knowledge and reads like a philosophy of science text most of the time (cf. Lötter 1994: 154). Lyotard distinguished between narrative and scientific knowledge as two distinct species of discourse which can both fulfil legitimate functions (1984: 29f.). He does claim, however, that narratives provide a certain kind of knowledge that cannot be had in any other way. This narrative knowledge can also function as a legiti-mation for scientific knowledge instead of the grand meta-narratives that previously legitimated science in the modern world (Lyotard 1984: 18ff.). But why would this postmodern view of knowledge be important for the theology and science dialogue in general, or for specific issues like reflecting on God's action in the world today?

Most of us would agree that the typically modernist view

of science found its apex in the positivistic view of science: here objective, true scientific knowledge is grounded in empirical facts which are uninterpreted, indubitable and fixed in meaning; theories are derived from these facts by induction or deduction and are accepted or rejected solely on their ability to survive objective experimentation; finally, science progresses by the gradual accumulation of facts (cf. J. W. van Huyssteen 1989: 3ff.; Jones 1994: 3). Postmodern science,[8] however, finds its best expression in postpositivist, historicist and even post-Kuhnian philosophies of science, which have revealed the theory-ladenness of all data, the underdetermination of scientific theories by facts, and the shaping role of epistemic and non-epistemic value-judgments in the scientific process. Postmodern philosophy of science also reveals the narrative and hermeneutical dimension of science to us by acknowledging that science itself is a truly cultural and social phenomenon (cf. Bernstein 1983: 30ff.). This not only results in the cross-disciplinary breakdown of traditional boundaries between scientific rationality and other forms of rational inquiry, but also in the inevitable move from being objective spectators to being participants or agents in the very activities that were initially thought to be observed objectively. Stephen Toulmin puts it succinctly: all postmodern science must start by reinserting humanity back into nature, and then integrate our understanding of humanity and nature with practice in view (cf. Toulmin 1985: 210; 237f.; 257). Epistemologically this is ultimately recognized as the turn from foundationalism to holism, but also as the move away from a modernist notion of indivi-

---

[8] According to Stephen Toulmin, the phrase 'postmodern science' was coined by Frederick Ferré (cf. Toulmin 1985: 210).

dualism to the indispensable role of the community in post-modern thought (cf. Murphy 1990: 201ff.).

Theologians who are engaged in serious dialogue with the sciences will find the postmodernist rejection of grand, legitimizing metanarratives and the seemingly complete acceptance of pluralism a formidable challenge for both theology and science. A crucial and increasingly controversial theme throughout the development of twentieth-century philosophy of science has been precisely the justification for interpreting the history of science in terms of a modernist story of progress or rational development (cf. Rouse 1991b: 610). Postmodern philosophy of science now challenges this ubiquitous notion of progress by its combination of respect for the local context of inquiry and resistance to any global interpretation of science that could constrain local inquiry. As such it refuses, along with many feminist critiques, any overall pictures or grand narratives that would want to explain science as a unified endeavour with an underlying essence: rather it makes sense of everyday science by seeing it as a set of narrative enterprises that work very well in quite specific circumstances (cf. Lötter 1994: 160). At the same time, of course, it also raises serious political issues by sharply focussing on the autonomy and cultural authority of the sciences. Postmodern philosophy of science, therefore, realizes that science must be understood as a historically dynamic process in which there are conflicting and competing paradigm theories, research programmes and research traditions (cf. Bernstein 1983: 171ff.). The postmodern attitude is also, however, part of a generally trusting attitude toward local contexts of practice, an attitude which asks us to trust scientific traditions, where these are understood not as a consensus of authority, but rather as a field of concerns within which both consensus and dissent acquire a local intelligibility (Rouse 1991b: 614). This important fact reveals that the reasons, arguments and value-judgments employed by communities of scientists are fundamentally related to, or 'grounded' in, social practices. The very criteria and norms that formerly seemed to guide scientific activity safely have thus become open and vulnerable to criticism.

Tradition and interdisciplinary reflection

In this argument for a postmodern science, then, we find a powerful call to return to the local context and to recognize the way tradition shapes the daily activity of the scientist in the workplace. But, is not this call to tradition in both postmodern theology and postmodern science in conflict with another one of postmodernism's strong tenets, namely its radical critique of any notion of progress and of any view that sees one discipline as having some kind of epistemological authority over another? Whatever notion of postmodernity we eventually may want to opt for, all postmodern thinkers certainly see the modernist quest for epistemic certainty, and the accompanying programme of laying foundations for our knowledge, as an impossible dream, a contemporary version of the quest for the Holy Grail (cf. Schrag 1989: 84). Postmodern thinkers from Michel Foucault to Richard Rorty have coupled exactly this deconstruction of the epistemological paradigm of modernist philosophy with a marked recognition of the contextual and the social resources of human rationality. On this view human reason no longer issues from an isolated, epistemic consciousness, but unfolds in a variety of sociopolitical functions in focussed attention toward the marginalized, that which is left out, and those who are constructed as the other (cf. Rossouw 1993: 902). Michel Foucault in particular, in his celebrated attack on a totalizing and hierarchical rationality, has made much of 'regimes of knowledge' as forms of social practices that reflect – consciously or unconsciously – certain power relations within the existing social order. For Foucault it is precisely tradition, and the perspective of progress and uninterrupted continuity that we project on to it, which preserves the power relations which underlie all conventions and oppressions (cf. Foucault 1989: 89). For Foucault power is the fundamental characteristic of human culture and tradition, and as such it also and always produces knowledge. But power and knowledge are so integrated with one another that there would be no point in dreaming of a time when knowledge will cease to depend on power: it is impossible for power to be exercised without knowledge, and it is impossible for knowledge not to engender power (cf. Foucault 1989: 52). What is clear, however, is his sharp criticism of all thinking which protects itself by retreating to the safe context of an ongoing, progressive tradition (cf. Byrne 1992: 335). In his own words:

> I adopt the methodical precaution and the radical but unaggressive scepticism which makes it a principle not to regard the point in time where we are now standing as the outcome of a teleological progression which it would be one's business to reconstruct historically (Foucault 1989: 49).

Clearly, one of the most distinguishing characteristics of the 'postmodern' is precisely the crisis of continuity which now disrupts the accepted relationship between an event and a tradition which gains its stability from that relationship. The writings of Michel Foucault offer a vivid picture of precisely the kind of postmodern thinking which seeks to purge history of any such overtones of metaphysical continuity (cf. Byrne 1992: 335). This view of tradition certainly presents a radical challenge to Christians who generally try to live in continuity with the event and person of Jesus Christ and for whom the relationship to this kind of tradition is based on the witness of scripture and the preaching and tradition of the church. By seeking to disturb any easy relationship with our past, arguing that our assertion of continuity is itself an invention of our need to control the destiny of our culture and society, sceptical forms of postmodern critique of continuity call into question the very possibility of tradition.

On the other hand, though, James Byrne has argued that even Foucault's anti-metaphysical critique – while stressing abrupt changes in history – never actually glorified discontinuity to the extent of denying the continuity of traditions completely (1992: 341). In fact, it should be possible to recognize both the continuity and discontinuity of traditions, and what is to be rejected is any claim to a necessary, modernist, or metaphysical continuity in history. In this sense tradition is not something which we can presume as an ontological datum, but is rather something we construct out of the phenomena of history. The same postfoundationalist awareness of the vulnerability and ambiguity of all traditions is found in Delwin Brown's carefully constructed theory of religious traditions. Brown also sees continuity and change as primary categories in the dynamics of tradition, and, by acknowledging that the behaviour of traditions is fundamentally pragmatic and has to do with survival, power and legitimation, he argues that tradition creates, sustains and recreates communal and individual entities (cf. D. Brown 1994: 24–8).

This opens up a door, beyond the postmodern crisis of continuity, to theologize with a tradition whose continuity no longer has to be guaranteed by a foundationalist metaphysics of history. In this way we are empowered to criticize our traditions while standing in them, but also to allow a particular history to speak for itself without being subsumed under the umbrella of an all-encompassing theory, based on a series of texts and interpretations which we have endowed with a particular authority and which then function as the accepted ideology of a specific community. On this view our traditions and also our research traditions – those interpretative sets of theories that we construct to make sense of the continuities and discontinuities of our traditions – thus do not have to represent a repressive consensus of authority, but can indeed rather be seen as a creative field of concerns within which both consensus and dissent, continuity and discontinuity, acquire coherence and intelligibility (cf. Rouse 1991b: 614).

In this very specific sense one can then say that the primary task of the critical theologian is to examine the tradition – not just to repeat it – and through critically examining the tradition to allow the present to be reshaped more closely along the lines of what the tradition truly stands for (cf. Byrne 1992: 347). But this critical engagement with one's own tradition or with other research traditions never happens in epistemic isolation. The postfoundationalist notion of theological rationality for which I am arguing here claims exactly the opposite: we should be able to enter into cross-contextual and interdisciplinary conversations with our strong personal convictions intact, but at the same time be theoretically empowered to reach beyond the boundaries and limitations of our own traditions and forms of life.

Along with the typical traits of a postmodern philosophy of science, it is now clear that postmodernism's general embracing of pluralism, and the resulting rejection of grand metanarratives that universally legitimize the cultural dominance of scientific thought, now indeed seem to have serious implications for the interdisciplinary location of theology and thus also for the theology and science discussion. The fundamental question, 'Is postmodern religious dialogue possible today?' (cf. Comstock 1989: 189ff.), now translates into an even more complex question: is any meaningful dialogue between postmodern science and postmodern theology possible, or does the pluralism and localization of postmodern discourse throw theologians, philosophers and scientists, who are supposed to share some common quest for human understanding, into near complete epistemological incommensurability? Disturbingly enough, some postmodern theologians seem to accept just this in their enthusiastic embrace of a postmodernism of reaction (cf. Hodgson 1989: 29) that calls for a 'postliberal' return to orthodox or neo-orthodox epistemic values and confessional traditions. This should again alert us to the fact that postmodernism is a complex phenomenon and that no position in either theology or philosophy of science – just because it claims to be postmodern – should be accepted uncritically.

For Christian theology the ultimate postmodern challenge to its rationality and its credibility as a belief system can be stated as follows: do we still have good enough reasons to stay convinced that the Christian message does indeed provide the most adequate interpretation and explanation of our experience of God, and of our world as understood by contemporary science? Put differently: does it still make sense within a postmodern context to be committed to the fact that our evolving, expanding universe, as we have come to know it through science, ultimately makes sense only in the light of Sinai and Calvary (cf. Berger 1979: 165)? We are indeed uncomfortable with the idea, whether it is loosely derived from the Bible or more strictly taken from reason, that the same universal principles undergird every particular conversation. This scepticism, I think, is well-founded, since too many of our conversations have in the past been decided in advance by our patriarchal, sexist, classist, or racist metanarratives. For 'pre-postmodernists' it apparently seems less complicated to strive for truth, to distinguish between right and wrong interpretations of the biblical text, or true and false propositions, and to maintain some form of objective moral truth. In a postmodern world, however, we worry about efforts to plan and build one world, one conversation for humankind, one story of humanity (Comstock 1989: 191). For the dialogue between theology and the sciences this has serious implications: if our trusted metanarratives can no longer be trusted to provide any basis for interdisciplinary conversation, how can they ever be trusted to open up a safe epistemological space for the dialogue between theology and the sciences (cf. J.W. van Huyssteen 1997a: 278)?

Towards an interdisciplinary duet for theology and science

The positive appropriation of some constructive forms of postmodern critique finds its main focus in what I have called postfoundationalism (cf. J.W. van Huyssteen 1997a; 1997b: 58off.). Postmodernist critique, as we saw, first of all implies a very pointed rejection of all forms of epistemological foundationalism, as well as those ubiquitous, accompanying metanarratives which so readily claim to legitimize all our knowledge, judgments, decisions and actions. Both in theology and philosophy of science, foundationalism is often rejected in favour of nonfoundationalism. Philosophically, non- or antifoundationalism can certainly be seen today as one of the most important roots or resources of postmodernism. Nonfoundationalists deny that we have any of these alleged strong foundations for our belief systems and argue instead that our beliefs all form part of a groundless web of interrelated beliefs. In a strong reaction against modernist and generic notions of rationality, nonfoundationalism also highlights the crucial epistemic importance of community, the fact that every community and context has its own rationality, and that any social activity could in fact function as a test case for human rationality. In its extremest form, nonfoundationalism will imply an radical relativism of rationalities and, in a move that will prove to be fatal for the interdisciplinary status of theology, will claim internal rules for different modes of reflection. This kind of relativism could be so complete that any attempt at cross-disciplinary conversation would seem to face near-complete incommensurability.

Over against the alleged objectivism of foundationalism and the extreme relativism of most forms of nonfoundationalism, postfoundationalism in theology and the sciences wants to:

first, fully acknowledge contextuality and the embeddedness of both theology and all the sciences in human culture;

second, affirm the epistemically crucial role of interpreted experience and the way that tradition shapes the epistemic and non-epistemic values that inform our reflection about both God and our world;

third, at the same time creatively point beyond the confines of the local community, group, or culture, towards a plausible form of interdisciplinary conversation;

fourth, find the epistemological warrant for this interdisciplinary conversation in the biological sources of human rationality.

Postfoundationalism can therefore be seen as a viable third epistemological option beyond the extremes of objectivism and relativism, of foundationalism and nonfoundationalism. The postfoundationalist move in theology and science will therefore be held together by a two-fold concern: first, recognizing that we always come to our cross-disciplinary conversations with strong beliefs, commitments, and even prejudices; and second, identifying the shared resources of human rationality in different modes of reflection, which allows us to reach beyond the walls of our own epistemic communities in cross-contextual, cross-cultural and cross-disciplinary conversation.

The postmodern challenge in theology and science has revealed quite clearly that both modernism and postmodernism, as contemporary cultural phenomenona, have been unable to come to terms with the issue of rationality in any positive way. As a result of this, as we saw earlier, nearly all of the stereotyped ways of relating theology and science through models of conflict, independence, consonance, harmony, integration or dialogue are likely to be revealed as overly simplistic generalizations about the relationship between these two dominant forces in our culture (cf. J. W. van Huyssteen 1997b: 581). The challenge of postmodernist pluralism, however, not only implies a heightened awareness and historical sensitivity to the shifting boundaries between theology and the sciences, but also makes it virtually impossible even to speak so generally about 'rationality', 'science', 'religion', 'theology', and finally, 'God'. This necessitates, as we saw, an epistemological awareness of the fact that 'theology' and 'science', to begin with, never exist in such a generalized, abstract sense anyway, but always only in quite specific social, historical and intellectual contexts. A post-foundationalist notion of rationality is therefore embedded in this kind of historicization of scientific and theological projects. As such it clears an interdisciplinary space for thinking between more than one knowledge system or reasoning strategy, in what Sandra Harding has called a 'borderlands epistemology' (cf. Harding 1996: 15f.).

The postmodern mood in theology and science thus confronts us with serious and quite concrete challenges. Of great importance here would be the question whether our postmodern scepticism will allow us to continue trusting in our rational abilities and language somehow to interact with the world. It would also require asking whether postmodern religion can still provide us with a certainty of faith that will 'weigh us down', or whether we are doomed to 'the unbearable lightness of being postmodern' (cf. Percesepe 1991: 118ff.). I am convinced that, for the theology and science dialogue to have a purpose, and to be carried out meaningfully, we seriously need to try to find answers to these questions. A first step in the right direction will be to rule out one of the most important and influential misconceptions about postmodern thought, i.e., the assumption that it is always radically opposed to modern thought. Rather, it is important to view postmodern critique positively as an ongoing and relentless, critical return to the questions raised by modernity. From this perspective, postmodern thought is undoubtedly part of the modern, and not merely modern thought coming to its end. Seen in this way, the modern and the postmodern are also unthinkable apart from one another, because the postmodern shows itself best in the 'to-and-fro movement' between the modern and the postmodern (cf. Schrag 1992: 7).

For theology the shift to postmodern thought will immediately mean that central theological terms like religious experience, revelation, tradition and divine action can no longer be discussed within the generalized terminology of a metanarrative that ignores the socio-historical location of the theologian as an interpreter of experience and an appropriator of tradition. Within the context of a postmodern, holist epistemology, it will eventually also prove to be epistemologically impossible for theologians to continue seeing religious experience and tradition (which includes theological interpretations of revelation) dualistically as two opposing poles that somehow have to be related to one another (cf. Dean 1988: 20). Trying to think through the troubled and confused relationship between theology and science, as well as the complex sets of epistemic and non-epistemic values that shape the rationality of each, we might begin to realize that for the theologian willingly caught up in this dialogue postmodern faith need not be so 'heavy' and 'serious', and we can indeed readjust our thinking to resist the excessive 'weight' of any form of foundationalism, religious isolation or intellectual manipulation. This kind of epistemological fallibilism will not result in that one, maximally ideal, modernist knowledge system. Instead of one perfect representation of God, or of the world, however, it may yield for us a 'collage' of knowledge that aims to be the most reliable, the most useful, and the most meaningful we have (cf. Harding 1996: 22).

These views on trans-contextual, interdisciplinary conversation and evaluation are significantly strengthened when supported by the kind of postfoundationalist epistemology I have outlined above. It is also closely related to what Andy F. Sanders has recently called 'traditionalist fallibilism' (1995). According to this view tradition – not just cultural and religious tradition, but also the history of the evolution of human knowledge – is acknowledged, not just as part of our background knowledge, but as in fact the main source of our knowledge. In cross-contextual conversation the background of beliefs, commitments, and expectations – embedded in our traditions – is taken to be more than something merely on which to be worked, and as more than a common platform from which to start our inquiries. This 'more' consists in the trust in, and the reliance on, those traditions in terms of which we define our lives (cf. Sanders 1995: 206). This means not only that we practise our shared trades of theologies, the sciences, humanities and philosophy in the light of their respective disciplinary traditions, but also that we rely on a complex variety of epistemological, political, moral and religious traditions to define and shape our lives.

The fact that there are no longer any pre-set, foundationalist, universal, cross-cultural or interreligious rules for theology does not necessarily mean that all criteria are now always going to be only strictly local or exclusively contextual. If none of our criteria were to be acceptable beyond the boundaries of a research tradition, the giving of rational reasons beyond the boundaries of any tradition would be impossible (cf. D. Brown 1994: 6). The crucial problem for a theology located in interdisciplinary conversation therefore remains the following: is it at all possible to make sensible and rational choices between different viewpoints and alternative research traditions? At this point Larry Laudan's admonition to scientists and theologians comes to mind: unless we can somehow articulate criteria for choice between research traditions, we have neither a theory of rationality nor a theory of what progressive growth in knowledge should be (cf. Laudan 1977: 106). In theology, as in other forms of inquiry, providing warrants for our views thus becomes a cross-contextual obligation (cf. D. Brown 1994: 6f.).

Remarkable parallels are now surfacing here between theology and other modes of knowledge. A good example is again found in reasoning strategies as different as theology and the sciences: in both we are required to trust our traditions as we reach out beyond them in interdisciplinary conversation. In both theology and science we should be able to identify some criteria to warrant our theory choices, and neither scientific nor theological knowledge can ever claim demonstrably certain foundations for making these choices. Epistemic similarities between theology and the sciences do not mean, of course, that scientific knowledge is 'just like' theology, but they do mean that methods in science do not provide a uniquely rational and objective way of discovering truth. In both theology and science good arguments should therefore be offered for or against theory choice, or for or against the problem-solving ability of a research programme. Obviously, our good arguments and value judgments rest on broader assumptions and commitments which can always again be challenged. This does not mean, however, that any opinion is as good as any other, or that we can never compare radically different points of view (cf. Placher 1989: 51). What all of this does mean, however, is that we certainly are in need of a comprehensive epistemology that can somehow create an interdisciplinary space that would not be totalizing or universalist in the modernist sense of the word.

The postfoundationalist challenge always to critique our own assumptions certainly means that there are no universal standards of rationality against which we can measure other beliefs or research traditions. The fact that we lack a clear and 'objective' criterion for judging the adequacy or problem-solving ability of one tradition over another, does not, however, leave us with a radical relativism, or even with an easy pluralism. Our ability to make rational judgments and share them with various and different epistemic communities also means that we are able to communicate with one another meaningfully through conversation, deliberation and evaluation in an ongoing process of collective assessment. As we will see later, it is precisely the very ability to have even this kind of interdisciplinary conversation that will be vindicated by uncovering the sources of human rationality through a more comprehensive epistemology. Sharing our views and judgments with those inside and outside our epistemic communities could therefore lead to a real conversation, which we should enter not just in order to persuade, but also to learn. Such a style of inquiry can provide a way of thinking about rationality that respects authentic pluralism: it will not force us all to share the same assumptions, but it will find ways in which we can talk with one another and criticize our traditions while standing in them. In this sense genuine pluralism ought to allow for conversations between people who may enter them for very different reasons (Placher 1989: 117) and who in fact may disagree about many issues. This pluralism allows for a legitimate diversity: the fact that different people have different experiential situations because they come from a complex collage of different traditions makes it normal, natural and rational that they should often proceed differently in cognitive matters (cf. J. W. van Huyssteen 1997a: 38). But what holds the key to unlocking the shared sources of human rationality is exactly what we now have to pursue in these lectures. Amazingly enough, it will be in our tentative conversation with contemporary cosmology and the controversial theory of evolution by natural selection that we will find first the clues and then the solution to the elusive quest for a comprehensive epistemology that will yield the possibility of true interdisciplinary conversation.

This will eventually mean that, even if we lack universal rules for human knowlege and rationality, and even if we can never judge the reasonableness of statements and beliefs in isolation from their cultural or disciplinary contexts, we can still meaningfully engage in cross-contextual evaluation and conversation and give the best available cognitive, evaluative or pragmatic reasons for the responsible choices we hope to make. True interdisciplinary reflection in theology and sciences will therefore be achieved when our conversations proceed, not in terms of imposed 'universal' rules or meta-narratives, nor in terms of purely *ad hoc* contextual or local rules, but when we identify the safe space where both strong Christian convictions and the public voice of theology are fused in public conversation with the sciences. An acknowledgment of the pluralistic character of such an ongoing process of collective assessment should open our eyes to how the richness of our various traditions, communities, sciences and practices make up our social and intellectual domains and shape our behaviour as well as our different modes of intellectual understanding. Each of our domains of reasoning may indeed have its own particular logic and an understanding unique to its specialized domain, but in each the rich resources of human rationality are powerfully present. When we discover the shared richness of the resources of rationality without attempting to subsume all discourses under one universal reason, we have discovered the richness of the kind of interdisciplinary reflection which forms a natural space for a 'graceful duet' between theology and science.

The basic thesis of this lecture series, therefore, is that a constructive appropriation of some of the epistemological issues raised by the postmodern challenge to religion and science will make it possible, first, to collapse rigid, modernist disciplinary distinctions into a more comprehensive interdisciplinary space, where, second, traditional epistemic boundaries and disciplinary distinctions are blurred precisely because the same kind of interpretative procedures are at work in all our various reasoning strategies, and, third, through a creative fusion of hermeneutics and epistemology, reasoning strategies as distinctive and different as theology and the various social and natural sciences may be revealed to share the rich resources of human rationality. The dilemma for the philosophical theologian is, as we have seen, that both the historicist deconstruction of Western metaphysics and the aftermath of the collapse of all epistemological foundationalism have not only rendered the feasibility of any attempt at a comprehensive approach to human knowledge and rationality impossible, but have revealed the very possibility of public, interdisciplinary discourse as profoundly problematical. I will argue for the interdisciplinary status of theological reflection by showing that the possibility for a constructive postmodernist, comprehensive approach to the rationality of interdisciplinary reflection is supported by at least the following arguments:

First, true interdisciplinary reflection in theology will only be achieved in a postfoundationalist mode where the interdisciplinary conversation proceeds, not in terms of imposed 'universal' rules, nor by purely *ad hoc* rules, but in terms of the intersubjective agreements we reach through persuasive rhetoric and responsible judgment, and where both the strong personal convictions so typical of religious commitment, and the public voice of theology, are acknowledged in interdisciplinary conversation (cf. J. W. van Huyssteen 1998b).

Second, I will argue that theological reflection is radically shaped by not only its social, historical and cultural context, but also by the biological roots of human rationality. Especially in contemporary evolutionary epistemology we will find surprising, if not startling, attempts to facilitate precisely the challenge of a constructive form of postmodernism: the need for a more comprehensive and integrated approach to the problem of human knowledge. Evolutionary epistemology, rightly understood, will reveal the biological roots of all human rationality and should therefore precisely lead to an interdisciplinary account of our epistemic activities. As we will see in the fourth and final lecture, the basic assumption of evolutionary epistemology is that we humans, like all other living beings, result from evolutionary processes and that, consequently, our mental capacities are constrained and shaped by the mechanisms of biological evolution. I will accept, at least in a minimalist sense, that all our knowledge, including our scientific and religious knowledge, is grounded in biological evolution. And if human knowledge results from evolution, then the study of evolution will be of extreme importance for an understanding of the phenomenon of knowledge, and therefore also directly for epistemology. I will also show why evolutionary epistemology meets the need for facilitating a postfoundationalist notion of rationality that takes us beyond traditional disciplinary boundaries. Evolutionary epistemology, rightly understood, will therefore facilitate an interdisciplinary account of all our epistemic activities. In the light of my arguments for this thesis, I will argue that Darwin (and neo-Darwinism) was right in arguing that metaphysical and religious beliefs in humans are related to evolutionary processes, and that human rationality therefore has strong biological roots. I will also argue, however, that although this may explain away deistic notions of God, it does not fully explain religious belief, and certainly not theism as such.

Conclusion

In our search for a comprehensive epistemology, we will focus especially on some of the sensational discoveries in contemporary cosmology and evolutionary biology. Historically, the theology and science debate has certainly been shaped decisively by the profound and ultimate questions raised for theology by these important sciences. One of the most remarkable links between theology and science today is found between physics, cosmology and theology: the possibility (or not!) of a new form of natural theology, frowned upon earlier this century by most theologians, now seems to have been taken up again by physicists like John Polkinghorne, cosmologists like Stephen Hawking and Paul Davies, and bio-chemists like Arthur Peacocke. Many now seem to think that physics – and in a broader sense, cosmology – is actually quite compatible with some sort of monotheism (cf.Rolston 1996: 62f.). As we will see, one of the most important factors adding to this belief has been the anthropic principle in cosmology: we now know that this universe originated some 12 to 15 billion years ago in a 'Big Bang' and that it has since been expanding. From this primal burst of energy, elementary particles formed, and afterwards hydrogen, the simplest element, served as fuel for the stars, where the heavier elements were forged.

In retrospect, it can now indeed seem that the universe has been 'fine-tuned' from the start for the subsequent construction of stars, planets, life, and, as we will see, ultimately the human mind. And Holmes Rolston is right: a plausible interpretation for many here indeed seems to be some form of divine design. However, theologians and philosophers have rightly been wary of design arguments, remembering Paley, his fine-tuned watch, and the many important criticisms of such arguments (cf. Rolston 1996: 63). Yet our physical world seems to be resembling a fine-tuned watch again, and now many new and plausible arguments seem to support the argument for some form of design: we find a single blast (the Big Bang) fine-tuned to produce a world that produced us, when any of a thousand other imaginable blasts would have yielded nothing. From this Rolston has drawn an important conclusion: theologians and scientists alike may find it perfectly intelligible to draw conclusions that may be consistent with religious faith from a fine-tuned universe, though theistic (or monotheistic) conclusions are certainly not the only ones that can be drawn. In fact, nothing in Christianity implies the detail of the Big Bang theory. Also, many other cosmologies could be compatible with Christian faith in creation (1996: 64).

A Safe Space for Theology and Science?

As we will see in the next chapter, it really is difficult to imagine a universe much less staggering, dramatic and mysterious, for all its rationality and intelligibility, than our universe. Even more fascinating, however, is the fact that contemporary cosmology argues for treating the observable universe as a single object, which therefore implies that the universe must somehow have intelligibility as a single object of study. Exactly this point will be our cue as we proceed to search for the kind of comprehensive epistemology that might yield the interdisciplinary nature of this mode of knowledge. And as we will discover, it is exactly in this sense that not only evolutionary epistemology, but also contemporary cosmology may offer a positive response to the postmodern disillusionment with all totalizing forms of knowledge. Our conversations with both cosmology and evolutionary biology may therefore succeed in pointing the way to the kind of comprehensive epistemology that might actually enhance and elucidate our interdisciplinary reflection without subsuming it under the dominance of ideological metanarratives.

But is there a way towards such a comprehensive form of human knowledge that would not be vulnerable to the postmodern disillusionment with all totalizing and universalizing forms of knowledge? I believe that an important pointer towards such a postfoundationalist view will be found in the fact that theology and cosmology, although widely diverse as reasoning strategies, are both essentially interdisciplinary in nature, and as such share deeply in the quest for a more comprehensive and interrelated knowledge of the origin, the meaning and the destiny of our universe. I also believe that precisely the fact that contemporary cosmology explicitly argues for treating the observable universe as a single object implies that in some way or the other the universe must have at least some form of intelligibility as a single object of study. This almost necessarily presupposes and implies a kind of comprehensive epistemology that would reflect precisely the interdisciplinary nature of this mode of knowledge.

Not only in cosmology, however, but also in evolutionary epistemology, we will find persuasive arguments for the emergence of exactly such a comprehensive view of human knowledge. As will become clear later, evolutionary episte-mology will reveal a quite remarkable ability to facilitate and embrace this quest for a comprehensive account of human knowledge, a quest already so alive and well in theology and cosmology today. Of utmost importance will also be the fact that our universe essentially is an evolving universe. From the standpoint of contemporary science, the whole history of the universe is in fact a history of evolution. On our planet, that process of evolution has continued, as simple atoms of carbon, hydrogen, oxygen and other elements built up and developed into the millions of life-forms that now exist on earth. That such a process has taken place is one of the foundations of contemporary modern science. In fact, the idea of evolution itself has now become a theory with tremendous explanatory force, a theory that explains many otherwise puzzling features of our world in a very elegant way (cf. Ward 1996: 61).

So, looking backward from where we are today, we dis-cover what Holmes Rolston has called a pregnant earth, a primitive planetary environment in which the formation of living things had a high probability (cf. Rolston 1996: 65). And looking forward to the next century and millenium it is difficult to imagine that our evolutionary natural history will ever be less startingly fertile and prolific. Again Rolston is sharp and to the point: the dialogue between biology and religion will increasingly try to figure out whether in the genesis of these riches we need interference by a supernatural agency, or the recognition of a marvellous endowment of matter with a propensity towards life (1996: 66). Rolston is also correct in realizing that, even if a watchmaker-design type of notion for God may be intriguing for cosmologists to speculate about, it will not prove to be an appropriate model for biology, where more autonomy and self-creativity will have to be combined with God's will for life, a process of 'divine parenting' somehow entwined with the spontaneous, creative process of nature (1996: 66).

Rolston has also intriguingly predicted that in the century to come science will reveal the order achieved on our earth to be even more remarkable still, and that the biological sciences will continue both to support and to undermine it (1996: 67). That will most certainly ensure an active and ongoing dialogue between biology and theology about the ultimate source of our world's creative ordering, about the origin of life, and ultimately about the emergence of human consciousness. As we will see in the third chapter, prominent and outspoken biologists are continuing to chant 'chance, chance, chance', while what in fact has irrevocably resulted is order-increasing in complexity and sophistication, millennia after millennia. Therefore, the astounding drive that really needs explanation is what transforms chance into order, as creatures emerge and exploit the opportunities in their environment and are themselves transcended by later-coming, more highly ordered, more dazzling forms and dynamic processes (cf. Rolston 1996: 67).

In the fourth and final chapter we will see that late in the story of evolution human beings arrive. On the one hand,

37

their large brains are to be expected since intelligence conveys obvious survival advantage. On the other hand, this is not so obvious, since all the other five million or so presently existing species survive well enough without advanced intelligence, as did all the other five billion or so species that have come and gone over the millennia. Rolston again states this well: it is a fact, however, that in only one of these myriads of species does a transmissible culture develop, and in this one it develops explosively, with radical innovations. There is only one line that leads to persons, to self-awareness and consciousness, but in that line at least the steady growth of cranial capacity makes it difficult to think that intelligence was not being selected for. And with this growth, evolution by natural selection passed over into something else, and nature transcended itself in culture (cf. 1996: 69).

Finally, with human consciousness and culture, radically new elements like conscious experiences have come into existence and, as we will see, along with thoughts have also come values and purposes and ultimately a propensity for rational knowledge. It is precisely in an attempt to understand our own ability to cope intelligently with an increasingly intelligible world through knowledge that the impact of the theory of evolution is felt far beyond the boundaries of biology. Because of this in these lectures I will also and especially focus on the important discipline of evolutionary epistemology. My claim will be that evolutionary epistemology not only yields the kind of postfoundationalist, comprehensive epistemology that had eluded us in a sceptical postmodernist context, but might actually help us to rediscover the resources of human rationality that I believe are shared so deeply by both theology and science. I will argue that our theological reflection is radically shaped not only by its social, historical and cultural context, but also by the biological roots of human rationality. In contemporary evolutionary epistemology, then, we will find surprising and exciting attempts to facilitate precisely the challenge of a constructive form of postmodernism: the need for a more comprehensive and integrated approach to the problem of human knowledge. And by revealing the biological origins of all human rationality, evolutionary epistemology could possibly point the way to precisely the safe kind of epistemological space we would require for a graceful interdisciplinary duet between theology and the sciences.

Religion and Cosmology

Who are the High Priests of our Culture?

The fact that religion and science are both such influential, if not dominating, forces in our culture does not at all guarantee that there are easy and uncomplicated ways available for us today as we try to bring them into a meaningful conversation with one another. We now also know how unambiguously the history of science has revealed constantly shifting boundaries between theology and science (cf. Brooke 1991: 16ff.). The resulting ambiguities of history have furthermore been complicated today by the complete fragmentation of much of our attempts at knowledge in a postmodern world. As a result of this, it should now be quite clear that the difficult question, how two dominant cultural forces like religion and science relate to one another, can hardly be answered only with quaint and uncomplicated images like partaking in a 'duet' or engaging in a 'duel'. Of these two images, the idea of a 'duet' between theology and science possibly contains the richer resources, which we now have to start exploring. Moreover, the question of the relationship between theology and science is itself, of course, neither a proper theological nor a truly scientific question. It does, rather, point to a quintessentially epistemological problem, i.e., the philosophical challenge to try to figure out how two very different reasoning strategies, and two sets of very different claims to knowledge, are to be related to one another (cf. McMullin 1981: 26). What is at stake here is basically the nature and origin of human knowledge and the way it presents itself in the often very divergent claims resulting from distinct religious or scientific world views. I therefore believe that the basic human conviction that our complicated and often very mysterious world is also highly intelligible should also motivate us to search intensely for at least some plausible, comprehensive theory of human knowledge. There is no way that we could be content with a plurality of unrelated language games if they are in fact languages about the same world – especially if we are seeking a coherent interpretation of all our experience (cf. Barbour 1990: 16).

In the search for the kind of comprehensive epistemology that might create a safe interdisciplinary space for the theology and science dialogue in our postmodern world, I will assume and presuppose some of the most salient features of the current discussion on theology and science. John Polkinghorne recently voiced these features as the five principal concerns that have characterized the conversation between theology and science over the past thirty years (cf. Polkinghorne 1998: xi), and I will restate them as follows: the theology and science discussion in our time has been characterized, first, by a rejection of reductionism and a new awareness of the hermeneutical dimension of science; second, by a fairly pervasive understanding of the evolutionary universe as compatible with the Christian theological doctrine of creation; third, by a revival of what many are calling a new theology of nature, or a cautiously revised form of natural theology; fourth, by the realization that theology and science share in a mutual quest for intelligibility; and fifth, by an ongoing reflection on how physical processes might be sufficiently open to accommodate the acts of agents, both human and divine.

In our attempt to construct a postfoundationalist world view that would incorporate both theological and scientific perspectives, the obvious question is therefore going to be: what is the status of scientific claims about our cosmos, and what sort of knowledge claims, if any, do we make in theology? If, furthermore, a religious world view claims any form of 'revelation' as the basis for theological knowledge claims, what kind of knowledge are we talking about here? What is more, is it at all possible – or even desirable – that our preferred theological perspectives may be able to assist us, for instance, in choosing between different scientific theories that may be more or less compatible with biblical world views and thus transform the deadly duel to a romantic, graceful dance or duet?

The complexity of these issues is very well illustrated when, for a moment, we briefly look at the history of the relationship between scientific cosmology and the Christian doctrine of creation (cf. J.W. van Huyssteen 1997a: 221f.). At the beginning of the early medieval period Jews, Christians and Muslims were agreed on at least one theological 'given': the universe had a beginning in time. This, of course, was based on the Genesis story of the creation, and Augustine, who in principle was willing to take the road of metaphor to avoid any conflict with 'demonstrated truths', was keen to show that there was no conflict here: God's creation was seen as a single timeless act through which time itself came to be (cf. McMullin 1981: 28). The rediscovery of Aristotle, however, first in Islam and then in the Latin West, introduced a new challenge to the doctrine of creation. Aristotle argued strongly that neither matter nor time could have a beginning. This led to a serious confrontation between a 'pagan' cosmology and Christian theology which, as Ernan McMullin has convincingly argued, brought about the most serious intellectual crises the church had faced in almost a thousand years (1981: 29f.). In 1215 the Fourth Lateran Council proceeded to attack the Aristotelian position and defined it as a doctrine of faith that the universe indeed had a beginning in time. Later, Thomas Aquinas would show that neither side of the debate could really be demonstrated philosophically. With the coming of the so-called 'new science' in the seventeenth century, however, the terms of the debate changed as Newton's mechanics appeared to allow for a compromise position: the absolutes of space and time were without beginning, but also without content. Creation meant that God brought matter to be within the confines of space at a finite time in the past.

However, the numerous traces of historical development on the earth's surface (eventually followed by the establishment of geology as a new science at the University of Cambridge in 1870) and the discovery later of the second law of thermodynamics made the Aristotelian notion of an unchanging, eternal cosmos seem quite implausible (cf. McMullin 1981: 30). Even later Einstein's general theory of relativity, combined with Hubble's 1929 discovery of the galactic red-shift, led to the widely acclaimed postulate of an expanding universe, or the so-called Big Bang theory, according to which a singularity is postulated about 12 to 15 billion years ago from which the expansion of our universe began. The importance of the Big Bang theory is easily recognized: for the first time physics was led by its own resources to something that sounded like a beginning of time (cf. Drees 1990: 17ff., 211ff.). This was followed by widely diverse theological responses that ranged from positions like that of Pope Pius XII, who hailed the theory as unqualified support for the Christian idea of creation, to complete rejection because it either looked too much like creation or conflicted with the fundamentalist or literalist notion of a creation that supposedly happened just a few thousand years ago. It would very soon become clear, however, that none of these positions take the complexities of the relationship between scientific and theological epistemology into consideration at all. As we will see, not only can the Big Bang not automatically be assumed to be either the beginning of time or of the universe, but it can also not be taken for granted that the lapse of time since the so-called Big Bang is necessarily the age of our universe (cf. McMullin 1981: 35). As we now turn towards some of the fascinating issues raised by contemporary cosmology, Stephen Hawking's famous question 'Did the universe have a beginning, and what is the nature of time?' (cf. Hawking 1988: 1) will therefore have to be very carefully defined, both scientifically and theologically. But in the same careful way we will have to realize that the theological intent of, for instance, the Genesis passages is to underline the dependence of an intelligible and contingent universe on a Creator and not necessarily to specify a first moment in time, at least in the technical sense of contemporary cosmology.

This brief example from the history of Western thought should already alert us to the epistemological fallacy of too directly and too easily inferring from contemporary science to theological doctrine. As we will see, it would be a serious mistake to take epistemological short cuts directly from, for example, the Big Bang to creation, from field theory to the Spirit of God, from chance to providence, from entropy to evil, or from the anthropic principle to design. The Big Bang model, for instance, does not entitle us to infer – theologically or scientifically – an absolute beginning in time. On the other hand, there is nothing inadmissible, either scientifically or philosophically, about the idea that an absolute beginning might have occurred. And if it did occur, it might indeed appear to be much like the horizon-event described by the Big Bang theory. But to take an epistemological short cut and eventually describe this horizon-event as the 'moment of God's creation' would be to explain it in terms of a cause that would not be scientific any more. In this kind of unreal world theologians may think they are part of an exciting 'equal opportunity duet', but scientists would most certainly be duelling with them (to overextend our metaphor one more time!).

Those of us who are theologians, then, have to be very aware of the natural boundaries of our own discipline. But we certainly also need to be aware of how reluctantly most scientists would approach any attempt at an interdisciplinary conversation between theology and the sciences. Much has been written about the almost natural inclination of many scientists to eschew religious explanations for reality. Scientists too are often drenched in a modernist culture where they end up operating with at least some of the following powerful assumptions (cf. Lötter 1997: 4ff.):

First, many scientists – and philosophers of science – still assume that it is possible to reconstruct 'the' scientific method and then to give a unitary explanation of how science progresses through an ongoing accumulation of empirically verified knowledge. In this typically modernist search for a unifying scheme, science is very often seen as a single intellectual enterprise with one method for all disciplines and research projects. As we saw in the previous chapter, the postmodern challenge to science has made this kind of passion for providing science with some universal meta-narrative, or unitary explanation for how science works, impossible. Not only has 'science' been transformed to highly local scientific practices, but no adequate overview of today's multitude of highly specialized scientific disciplines and research fields can be contained any more within one over-arching methodological domain called 'science' (cf. Lötter 1997: 4).

Second, many scientists and philosophers of science in this century also assumed that any rational reconstruction of scientific method and progress had to be based on the example of physics, if only because of its outstanding theoretical and technological successes in our time. In a postmodern context, however, no clear reason remains why physics should still be seen as a paradigm case of empirical science: in spite of their necessary interconnectedness, each science has its own group of experts, its specific body of knowledge, and its own techniques, methods, etc. (cf. Lötter 1997: 5).

Third, because of the pervasive notion of the superiority of physics, many scientists and philosophers of science assumed that physics should be normative for all other disciplines as well. We now know, however, that the adherence to this kind of faith in the superiority of natural scientific rationality has been severely challenged – if not destroyed – by the post-modern challenge to all the reductionist scientisms of our time.

In the light of these complicating factors, what kind of

conversation can a theologian now expect from the natural sciences, and specifically from physics and cosmology? What could a theologian rightly infer from the highly successful results of contemporary physics, and from the resulting spectacular cosmological theories? To try to answer these highly charged questions, we have to take a closer look at what contemporary cosmology really is about.

Shall we dance? or, Why cosmology and theology share a dream

Contemporary cosmology embraces a variety of scientific disciplines and addresses a wide range of unresolved fundamental issues concerning the character, structure, origin, and even the destiny of the universe. This fact accounts for the distinct interdisciplinary character of all cosmological reflection: it is indeed rarely clear in cosmological research and discussion where strictly scientific analysis ends and philosophical, or metaphysical, reflection begins (cf. Stoeger 1988: 219). It is precisely because of the vagueness as to what the actual limits of cosmology as a discipline are, that cosmology seems to have subtle but very important implications for theology and philosophy. What these implications are, and how they reveal important similarities between some of the questions and perspectives that cosmology and theology share, will soon become clear. As intellectual disciplines, theology and cosmology are both essentially interdisciplinary in nature, and as such they both also share in a mutual quest for a comprehensive knowledge of the origin, meaning and destiny of our universe. For this reason William Stoeger has rightly argued that some of the principal features of cosmo-

47

logy, its assumptions and conclusions, set the stage, as it were, for a critical, interdisciplinary conversation with philosophy and theology (cf. 1988: 219).

Also in contemporary evolutionary epistemology, as we will see later, there are strong arguments today for a comprehensive view of human knowledge, which will resonate closely with this quest for an interdisciplinary account of knowledge in theology and cosmology. Contemporary cosmology argues for treating the observable universe as a single object, and therefore implies that the universe has intelligibility as a single object of study. This will also imply a comprehensive epistemology that reflects the interdisciplinary nature of this mode of knowledge. In this sense both evolutionary epistemology and contemporary cosmology may offer a positive response to the postmodern disillusionment with all totalizing forms of knowledge, and may succeed in pointing the way to a comprehensive epistemology that might actually still enhance and elucidate our interdisciplinary reflection without subsuming it under the dominance of ideological metanarratives.

Cosmology's principle object is very specifically the observable universe as a single object; i.e., it focusses on the origin, the evolution and the structure or physics of observable physical reality as a single object of inquiry, with its own specific intelligibility (cf. Stoeger 1988: 219). Cosmologists now know that the universe is indeed expanding, and as in their quest for intelligibility they move back towards the Big Bang, the issues cosmology confronts become even more fundamental and basic, if not philosophical. Crucial, defining questions thus become part of cosmology's task: how are the four forces of the universe related to one another at the beginning? How did they become differentiated, and when?

What are the different families of fundamental particles at different energies which interact through these interactions? How does the continuum of space-time arise from the quantum unified field theory processes? What determines the arrow of time? Is entropy involved in this definition? And what is the origin of the laws of physics, which govern all these fundamental processes? These are some of the fundamental questions that cosmologists grapple with as they try to understand the very early phases of the observable universe (Stoeger 1998: 220).

When theology now joins the interdisciplinary conversation with cosmology, all these fundamentally important questions take on a rather different aura. The basic question, however, as we turn to this interdisciplinary conversation between theology and cosmology, is the following: how can we think of the universe, or the cosmos, as God's creation? By just asking this question in an interdisciplinary mode, theologians have to take seriously the Big Bang theory which now is almost regarded as orthodox cosmology and most certainly seems to command the greatest attention among cosmologists and physicists. What makes Big Bang cosmology so intriguing for (Christian) theologians is, first of all, the fact that Big Bang cosmology presupposes historical time and therefore suggests the possibility of an original beginning with an accompanying eschatology (cf. Peters 1989: 45). Secondly, and possibly more significantly, there is Big Bang cosmology's mood of contingency: our universe did not have to become what it is. For many, both of these important issues seem to suggest that science has discovered something that looks a lot like the Christian notion of creation (cf. Barbour 1989: 120ff.). Obviously this will always take us back to the original tricky question: what is the proper relationship between contemporary cosmology and the Christian-theological understanding of creation?

So what do we mean when we talk about Big Bang cosmology? According to this theory, about 12 to 15 billion years ago an explosion took place at an extremely small epicentre, and the entire universe today represents fragments of that explosion still flying through space (cf. Peters 1989: 47). In 1929, Edwin Hubble, examining the 'red shift' of light from distant nebulae, formulated what we now know as Hubble's Law: the velocity of recession of a nebula is proportional to its distance from us (cf. Barbour 1989: 116). We are therefore indeed part of an ever-expanding universe, and scientific data during the last decade of scientific research have produced evidence that confirms, or at least refines, this theory of an expanding universe. Complementary research in cosmology and physics has now led to the strong hypothesis that at the point of the 'bang' the universe was completely simple, and completely unified: this is literally the point before time ($t = o$), a singularity that we can say virtually nothing about, and where the laws of physics seem to break down completely.

In the equations which cosmologists usually use to model the universe, $t = o$ in most models represents this singularity, or initial singularity, now universally called the 'Big Bang'. William Stoeger has argued correctly that in a sense the Big Bang can be called the beginning of the universe. However, because it is a singularity, it is not clear what it really represents or what actually occurred: the model of which it is part most probably breaks down before the singularity is reached. This becomes even more clear from the point of view of quantum field theory: before the singularity is reached, the effects of quantum gravity will dominate and determine the space-time structure, and for technical reasons we are not at a point at which such quantum effects can even be properly included in our theories (cf. Stoeger 1988: 222). Furthermore, even if the singularity did represent what actually occurred, it is not an origin or a beginning in an absolute sense, and any possible state prior to the singularity is inaccessible to us. Long before reaching it, we will gradually lose our ability to make observations or perform experiments which directly test these extreme epochs. Because of the fact that the very laws of nature here cease to exist, this is the point where we reach the limits of scientific rationality.

According to the Big Bang theory, our universe therefore started out very hot and has been cooling off ever since. When the temperature decreases past a certain threshold, a so-called freezing out takes place: each freezing out involves the appearance of new forms of matter and energy. At the very hot beginning there were no molecules or atoms; the objects of nature, as well as the laws that govern them, were thus gradually produced (cf. Peters 1989: 48). In the expansion and cooling off after the Big Bang, the cooling matter eventually condensed and collected into galaxies and smaller planets like our earth. In Ted Peters' words:

> We on earth today are still riding one piece of shrapnel out and away from the point of initial explosion. But where are we going? What does the future hold? (Peters 1989: 51).

This image, of course, assumes that we live in an open universe. Cosmologists, however, differ about whether the expanding universe will for ever be 'open', or whether it may be 'flat' or 'closed'. Instead of expanding indefinitely, our universe just may actually collapse again (cf. Peters 1989: 51f.):

what happens will in fact depend on the density of the matter of the universe. The critical point is that quantity of mass necessary to slow down or stop this process of expansion. Should we have just the right amount, our universe would acquire just the right kind of balance to be called 'flat'. But if the density is greater than that which is necessary for a flat universe, the gravitational pull may draw everything back again and ultimately cause our universe to collapse, which is what cosmologists would call a 'closed universe'. The work of Ilya Prigogene and others in thermodynamics has also shown that time moves only in one direction, from the past to the future (the so-called 'arrow of time'), and that this arrow of time – whether cosmological or psychological – is in fact irreversible. Parallel to this is the Second Law of Thermodynamics, or Entropy, which directly implies that everything is subject to gradual dissolution and disintegration. The Second Law in principle also implies that the world, and things around us, will not go on for ever. This dovetails neatly with the standard Big Bang theory: according to this model, there is no everlasting future for intelligent living beings or even for the laws of nature as we know them:

– in a closed universe everything will be destroyed in the reheating of the Big Crunch;

– in an open universe everything will dissipate or break up into cold inertness;

Therefore, in Ted Peters' vivid, dramatic language: 'whether fried or frozen, all life will end' (Peters 1989: 53).

This apocalyptic scenario reveals another of the most important features of contemporary cosmology: it essentially describes our universe as an evolving universe. From an initial singularity, the universe exploded into movement and time, exploding to create three-dimensional space and rapidly cooling to form the elements of hydrogen and helium, which make up the great majority of elements in this universe. Stars ultimately formed from the hydrogen and helium atoms and, as they aged, exploded to form carbon, the basis of all life-forms. From the formation of planetary systems, various elements such as carbon, hydrogen, nitrogen and many others combined to form the very finely balanced environment capable of originating and sustaining organic life-forms (cf. Ward 1996: 61). From this clearly flows why it will be important later to place the theory of evolution by natural selection, and also trends in contemporary evolutionary epistemology, within the broader context of the evolution of our universe. Keith Ward states it well:

> From the standpoint of modern science, the whole history of the universe is a history of evolution, of the development of complex structures out of simple elements, in ,accordance with in-built principles of interaction, the 'laws of physics'. On this planet, that process of evolution has continued, as simple atoms of carbon, hydrogen, oxygen and other elements built up and developed into the millions of life-forms that now exist on earth. That such a process has taken place is one of the foundations of modern science, and the idea of evolution explains many otherwise puzzling features of our world in a very elegant way (1996: 61).

William Stoeger, too, has pointed to the fact that evolution certainly is obvious on small and intermediate astronomical scales like stars, clusters of stars, galaxies and clusters of galaxies. The fact of microwave background radiation is a clear indicator, however, that there was a succession of hotter, denser phases, and that there was a time when the universe as a whole was homogeneous on relatively small scales. As expansion and cooling proceeded, complexification on many levels occurred to give us the hierarchical structuring we observe today (cf. Stoeger 1988: 222). From this very clear and evident process of evolution it follows that the universe must have both a physical origin or starting point, but also an end point or future with certain definite characteristics: depending upon the amount of matter it contains, it will either expand for ever, or it will recollapse (cf. Stoeger 1988: 222).

From this brief discussion it has already become clear what kind of linguistic and epistemological problems may arise when cosmology and theology, although both essentially interdisciplinary in nature, start communicating with one another. Certain key words may have different meanings in cosmology, philosophy and theology (cf. words like universe, time, space, cause, etc.), and unfortunately we rarely, when discussing a particular issue within an interdisciplinary context, make these crucial linguistic distinctions adequately (cf. Stoeger 1988: 231). But even more important are the epistemological differences between the specific focus, experiential dimensions and the heuristic structures of these very different disciplines. Stoeger has very convincingly argued that, instead of identifying the difference between theology and cosmology as a difference between their focus on different objects (for instance, a focus on empirical problems vs. divine mystery), what we should emphasize, rather, is precisely their important differences in focus, experiential ground, and heuristic structures (cf. 1988: 232ff.). The focus as well as the experiential context of our disciplinary reflection thus becomes theological when we attend primarily to how believers experience the presence of God in their lives: it is this kind of interpreted religious experience that Christian believers have called revelation, or the presence of God, or divine action. Obviously, the communication of what Christians call 'revelation' will always be in terms of what lies on this side of our epistemic horizons, but its content, its significance and its focus may be deeply revelatory of what lies beyond them. Therefore, when we reflect on the experiences of genuine love, of permanent commitment, and on the realities they may intend, then we open up ourselves to the possibility of 'revelation' taking place in our lives (cf. Stoeger 1988: 138).

Because theology and cosmology often ask the same ultimate questions concerning the origin, history and the future of our universe and of our own place in this ongoing cosmic event, science can and should directly influence theology, and this influence happens when the results of scientific investigation or the methodologies of science directly impact on theology. The natural sciences also have a direct impact on theology through new images, perspectives, symbols and stories. These images, perspectives and new myths can either enhance and purify religion when properly relativized and integrated, or they can distort and even destroy it when they are not acknowledged and properly engaged by religion in its dialogue with science and scientific culture (cf. Stoeger 1988: 241). As far as cosmology and its specific impact on theology goes, Stoeger points to the fact that, first, theology has to take very seriously the general conclusions and findings of contemporary cosmology – that is, that the universe is as large and as old as it is, that this universe is evolving, that all that is within it has had a common physical origin in time, and that all it contains is explicable by the natural sciences (cf. 1988: 239). Very specifically, however, the cosmologist should be aware of the limits of scientific rationality and of scientific explanations in cosmology, and the fact that empirical justification or verification is in principle limited: there are certain things about the universe that we will most probably never know for sure, and certain questions about physical reality which cosmology will never be able to address. As a result of the very clear limitations of scientific rationality, there will most probably always be explanatory gaps in the scientific account of the evolutionary development of the universe. This is also the most important reason why any 'God of the gaps' form of explanation should always be avoided, and why, whenever gaps in our understanding occur in a specific scientific context, they should be left for the scientific disciplines themselves to fill. These gaps inevitably end up being bridged by science itself, because at its own level science is capable of providing adequate and complete explanations (cf. Stoeger 1988: 239).

As we now move closer towards an evaluation of the work of two of the most exciting cosmologists of our time, it already is clear why it would be so questionable, precisely at this point, to establish too direct a parallel between 'the beginning of time' in the Big Bang and 'the beginning of time' in the Christian doctrine of creation. It would be impossible for cosmology as a science to unveil – on scientific terms – a point of absolute beginning, before which nothing existed, before which time of any sort was not, which would as such somehow already require the direct and visible influence of God (cf. also Stoeger 1988: 240). The fact that cosmology might not be able to explain such an event does not of course mean that it might not have occurred. It does, however, mean that cosmology is not able to discover it as a religious event of immense theological importance. As we will see, the limits of scientific rationality therefore indeed seem to point beyond it to a deeper religious mystery.

Can we, then, say something positive about the relationship and compatibility of religion and cosmology (science)? First, religion and theology should maintain a radical openness to, and a critical acceptance of, the range, the evolution and the structure of the physical, biological, psychological and cultural reality which the sciences reveal to us. But is such a disciplinary openness and critical acceptance reciprocal? Should scientists be open to learn from the conclusions of philosophy and theology? Many scientists may not seem to think so, but as we will see, even if the sciences, and therefore also cosmology, are self-sufficient at their own level of reflection, it is only through a direct conversation with philosophy, and with theologians who are open to the amazing impact of contemporary cosmology on religion and faith, that the language, the models of reflection, and the world views of scientists will be sharpened and will benefit directly from the 'duet' with theology and philosophy. This is especially true for theology and cosmology, since both of these reasoning strategies have been revealed to be truly interdisciplinary in nature.

Successful science: can it also get rid of God?

Thinking about the beginning and end of the universe as we know it unavoidably brings us to the God-question. This is certainly true for theologians and scientists alike. The most famous example here may be the case of the British cosmologist Stephen Hawking. In his world-wide best-seller *A Brief History of Time,* Hawking fully recognizes the fact that the concept of an absolute beginning, which seems to be implied in the standard Big Bang model, may also for some necessarily imply the existence of some kind of God. The reason for this is found in the following: the mere notion of a 'beginning' means that there must be an edge or boundary to our cosmos, and then, of course, we would be forced to ask 'what' or 'who' lies beyond this edge (cf. Hawking 1989: 53f.). Hawking's cosmology essentially tries to avoid this question and argues that the cosmos may not have a beginning in time, in which case we would not be needing the God-hypothesis. To understand this argument we first need to realize that normally we think of time as something we can extrapolate backwards at least as far as the 'point' in time which we call the singularity, the 'hot, big bang' from which scientists believe the expansion of our universe began (cf. Peacocke 1993: 133). Hawking now goes beyond Einstein and states that the theories of relativity and quantum mechanics should be able to combine into a single theory of quantum gravity. This Grand Unified Theory would eventually imply that we might in fact be able to describe the universe in terms of a single mathematical model that would be determined by the laws of physics alone. And as Hawking famously stated:

. . . if we do discover a complete theory, it should in time be understandable in broad principle by everyone, not just a few scientists. Then we shall all, philosophers, scientists, and just ordinary people, be able to take part in the discussion of the question of why it is that we and the universe exist. If we find the answer to that, it would be the ultimate triumph of human reason – for then we would know the mind of God (Hawking 1990: 175).

Hawking's ambiguous statement about knowing the mind of God through an ultimate 'theory of everything' is a stark reminder of the revival of sorts in recent years of traditional arguments for (or against) God's existence – not so much in theology, however, but in physics and cosmology. More importantly, though, some of these arguments – and particularly those of Stephen Hawking 'against' God – will reveal significant discrepancies between the God discussed by physicists and cosmologists and the God of most contemporary theologians (cf, Worthing 1996: 38). In Hawking's case the problem of randomness, raised specifically by the discovery of the uncertainty principle in quantum physics, would play a crucial role in arguing against the necessity of God as a first creator. Werner Heisenberg's 1926 formulation of the uncertainty principle has, of course, raised profound questions about the physical world in which we live today. Ever since the work of Laplace, classical physicists have tended to believe in a deterministic universe – that is, a universe of which, in theory, if the precise state could be known at any given time, then its state at any other time, past or future, could be calculated. Such a doctrine of scientific determinism was, quite naturally, opposed by those who believed it restricted God's freedom to intervene in the world too much (cf. Worthing 1996: 42). Worthing has also correctly argued that, ironically, the uncertainty principle not only made room for some kind of 'intervention', but also opened the way for potentially serious challenges not only to arguments from design, but to the very notion of design itself: if the most elemental building blocks of our universe behave in an apparently random manner, then it becomes almost impossible to attribute the present order in our world to some form of design, let alone build an argument for design on such data (cf. 1996: 42). In spite of the disappearance of the image of God as the 'divine Clockmaker', presiding over a steadily ticking universe, however, the design argument continues to attract attention. The fine-tuning of our universe indeed seems to have required precise initial conditions for a universe capable of sustaining life to develop, and the question obviously is whether as such it has been designed in any way, or whether our universe and the way it is should rather be seen as a coincidence of incredible proportions (cf. Worthing 1996: 43).

For Stephen Hawking the most plausible answer is to be found in his theory of quantum gravity. This theory obviously incorporates the Heisenberg uncertainty principle, and now implies that we do not need to think of boundary conditions for space and time any more: there only is a space-time dimension which is finite, but which does not take us back to a point of zero, before which there was no time (cf. Peters 1989: 55). Hawking and Hartle, in their attempts to combine quantum theory with gravitational theory, were led to the idea that the further one goes back along the ordinary 'real' time scale, the more it has to be replaced by a new parameter which now also includes a mathematical 'imaginary' component. For Hawking then, using the concept of imaginary time leads to the disappearance of the distinction between time and space. Furthermore, this space-'time' proved to be finite in extent and yet have no singularities that formed a boundary or edge (cf. Peacocke 1993: 133). Now there would be no singularities at which the laws of nature broke down, and no edge in space-time at which one would have to appeal to God to set the boundary condition for space-time. This then is the reason why Hawking could state:

'The boundary condition of the universe is that it has no boundary.' The universe would be completely self-contained and not affected by anything outside itself. It would be neither created nor destroyed. It would just BE (Hawking 1990: 136).

In 1970 Hawking and Penrose had also proved that Einstein's theory is only an incomplete theory: it cannot tell us why the universe started off, because it predicts that all physical theories, including itself, break down at the beginning of the universe. General relativity, however, claims to be only a partial theory, so what Hawking's singularity theorems show is that there must have been a time in the very early universe when the universe was so small that one can no longer ignore the small-scale effects of the other great partial theory of our century, quantum mechanics:

At the start of the 1970's, then, we were forced to turn our search for an understanding of the universe from our theory of the extraordinarily vast to our theory of the extraordinarily tiny (cf. Hawking 1990: 51).

Now in general relativity, a singularity is a region of space-time in which the curvature becomes so strong that the general relativistic laws break down and the laws of quantum gravity take over. By the late 1970s Hawking had realized that general relativity is not valid at the moment of the Big Bang, because of the uncertainty principle, and he was exploring the combination of general relativity and quantum mechanics into a more comprehensive theory. This finally led to his famous 'No-Boundary Proposal': time and space are finite but are closed up on themselves without any boundaries or edges. If correct, this would mean there would be no singularities, and the laws of science would hold everywhere, including at the beginning of the universe. Thus Hawking tried to apply quantum theory to the singularity at the beginning of the universe, and here lies the basics of his quantum cosmology, where imaginary time can now be used to study the singularity at the Big Bang, since at its birth the universe was entirely within the quantum state. Hawking's Theory of Everything, his quantum cosmology, is thus based on this 'No Boundary Proposal'. Hawking was always disturbed by the idea that the laws of physics would break down at the singularity at the beginning of the universe. He therefore had to develop the No Boundary Proposal which removes the singularity at the beginning of the universe; and without this 'moment of beginning' there would be no need for a Creator (at least in his mind). To accomplish this, time then had to be divided into two components: real and imaginary time. Unlike real time, the imaginary component does not vanish at the Big Bang and the theory is thus useful at the singularity.

The startling theological implication of Hawking's proposal is, of course, that the universe needs no transcendent Creator to bring it into existence at zero time ($t = o$), nor does it need God to tune the laws of nature to carry out its (divinely appointed) evolutionary purpose (cf. Hawking 1990: 140; also Peters 1989: 55). Here, then, lies the biggest challenge for the Christian theologian: we will eventually have to decide exactly which God, or what kind of God, Hawking is rejecting. But it is already clear that the uncertainty principle here has serious implications for the idea of causation. In quantum theory, particles are no longer seen as having distinct and well-defined positions and velocities that are observable. Rather, it is now known that they are in a quantum state that is interpreted in a statistical way, with the result that position and velocity cannot be measured at the same time with unlimited precision. Or, as Mark Worthing puts it: quantum mechanics does not predict the observation of any definite single result. Rather, quantum mechanics predicts a number of possible results and tells us statistically how likely each of these is (cf. 1996: 49f.). Einstein's famous remark that 'God does not play dice' was clearly made in resistance to the kind of indeterminism that would result from the uncertainty principle of quantum mechanics. Indeterminism, as we all know today, has, however, clearly won the day, and Niels Bohr's principle of complementarity has become the standard interpretation of quantum mechanics. And Worthing is obviously right: if the behaviour of individual electrons and other small particles is unpredictable, then the entire causal chain on which the cosmological argument rests appears to break down. In a quantum physical world, therefore, the causal form of the cosmological argument for the existence of God would be patently invalid (cf. 1996: 50). But as we will see, this is no way addresses the question whether God actually exists or not. It simply means that thinking of God as a mere first cause is not only seriously deficient, but actually inaccurate.

This much, however, is clear: the kind of God Hawking is rejecting is a kind of God that would fit our contemporary cosmology and our current scientific theories, a God that is ultimately needed to explain whatever still remains unexplained in science. This, however, is the typical (deistic) God-of-the-gaps that by no stretch of the imagination qualifies as the God of the Christian faith. This kind of God seems to be only a philosophical, abstract, first cause, and provides us with a 'divine' explanation whenever scientists fail to give us a 'natural' explanation (cf. Peters 1989: 56f.). It is also, of course, a classic deistic notion of God, where God brings the cosmos into existence at the beginning and then leaves it to run according to its built-in natural laws. The Christian, theistic notion of God is, however, radically different: whatever God, as Creator of the universe, did at the beginning, God is still active and present today in the events and history of our universe.

A proper answer to Stephen Hawking will, therefore, first of all include a rejection of this deistic notion of God, but also the realization that for God to be recognized as Creator, it is not necessary for God to be tied down to one 'event' at the 'beginning' of the ancient past. God's creative work still goes on in the present and will also in the future. The importance of Hawking's challenge, however, should not be too easily overlooked: Hawking has seen correctly that cosmology cannot avoid entering the theological conversation. The question of the origin and the beginning of all things necessarily and inevitably leads beyond the limits of scientific rationality to the question of God. To be able to answer the question of how we might conceive of our universe as God's creation, we will have to push beyond Hawking's limited and rather primitive/naive concept of God to a more theologically sophisticated concept of God.

Hawking's proposal, therefore, does not necessarily imply the downfall of belief in God as a Creator in the face of modern science. First, not all physicists and cosmologists are as optimistic about the possibilities of a no-boundary condition as Hawking and even see it as overly metaphysical and speculative (cf. Worthing 1996: 54); second, precisely the so-called implications of a no-boundary condition for a Creator may actually be false: in fact, no convincing reason has been given why – even in a universe without a temporal beginning – the question of the existence of God would suddenly become meaningless. Joseph Życiński has recently argued convincingly that there need be no substantive conflict between Hawking's no-boundary model of creation and the traditional Christian doctrine of creation (cf. Życiński 1996: 283). So, even if the universe had no edge, no beginning in time, the question 'why this universe at all?' would still be enormously relevant. And this is a question that cannot be answered by any theory in cosmology or physics alone, however grandly unified. In the end Hawking therefore argues against a specific form of the cosmological argument based on a temporal first cause, and therefore also against a specific philosophical construct he is calling 'God'. And Worthing is right: Hawking overlooks the crucial fact that the existence of God is not bound to a particular understanding of an original creation, nor does he reveal any knowledge of the important theological distinction between *creatio ex nihilo* and *creatio continuans* (cf. 1996: 55).

Is God the mystery at the end of the universe?

We have seen that Hawking's model for a quantum creation out of nothing in fact revealed a sustained attempt to get rid of God in the name of a superior natural scientific rationality. We also saw, however, that Hawking's famous dictum, 'if there is no edge, then there is no need for a creator God', mistakenly – and rather naively – sees God only as a typical deistic God-of-the-gaps, an 'explanation' needed only because science has not yet managed to give us final answers on ultimate origins. For Hawking, any reference to a boundary or an edge to our universe would necessarily open up the kind of gap that would make it psychologically easier to search for some kind of supernatural explanation; and it was precisely this kind of methodological move that he wanted to prevent (cf. Życiński 1997: 5f.). But as we saw earlier, even if we were to ignore or move beyond the naiveté of Hawking's notion of God and accept the plausibility of his quantum cosmological argument, we would still be stuck with difficult and challenging questions like the following:

- Why does our universe exist?
- Where do the universal laws of physics come from?
- What is the status of these laws of nature, and are these particular laws so absolute that no alternative laws could be imagined?
- Why can we describe complex physical processes by using simple mathematical formulae?

These questions are obviously of crucial importance to science, but they cannot be answered by science alone.

One physicist who certainly goes beyond Hawking in trying to find an answer to these ultimate questions is Paul Davies. Davies finds the true miracle of nature in the ingenious and unswerving lawfulness of the cosmos, an amazing lawfulness that permits complex order to emerge from chaos, life to emerge from inanimate matter, and consciousness to emerge from life. It is this remarkable order and lawfulness of nature that has produced beings who not only ask great questions of existence, but who, through science 'and other methods of enquiry', are even beginning to find some answers (cf. Davies 1992: 34).

Paul Davies' most interesting, and most complete, attempt to develop this position is found in his well-known *The Mind of God: The Scientific Basis for a Rational World* (1992). In the beginning of this book Davies states:

> I should like to make my position clear at the outset. As a professional scientist I am fully committed to the scientific method of investigating the world . . . Generally science leads us in the direction of reliable knowledge (Davies 1992: 14).

Towards the end of the book, however, Davies is ready to admit the following:

> The search for a closed logical system that provides a complete and self-consistent explanation for everything is doomed to failure . . . Is there a route to knowledge – even 'ultimate knowledge' – that lies outside the road of rational scientific enquiry and logical reasoning? Many people claim there is. It is called mysticism (Davies 1992: 226).

In many ways these two quotations reveal a journey from one viewpoint to another (cf. H.F. van Huyssteen 1996: 1f.). Earlier, in his 1983 book *God and the New Physics,* Davies still argued from a strong and almost simplistic contrast between science and religion, which ultimately explained his reductionist use of scientific explanations to assess religious claims, his claim that science offers us a surer path to God than religion (1983: ix), and his choice for a concept of a 'natural God' who would be wholly within the universe, constrained by the laws of physics. This conscious choice against the God of religion, i.e., a supernatural God, acting on the world in defiance of natural laws (1983: 208), would stay with Davies as he set out in *The Mind of God* to push back the logic of natural scientific rationality as far back as it will go. Ironically, however, the 'mind of God', the why of it all, the ultimate explanation of existence, turns out to be unanswerable in terms of scientific methodology, and Davies has to conclude with 'the mystery at the end of the universe' (cf. 1992: 223ff.) and the fact that scientific explanations indeed seem to have very definite limitations.

Finally Davies suggests that it is through another form of knowledge, through mysticism, that we may eventually be able to gain some form of ultimate knowledge (1992: 226). Davies' argument for an alternative mode of knowledge, an understanding of the universe and its existence and properties that lies outside the categories of scientific thought, is ultimately revealing for the title of his well-known book: *The Mind of God* comes from the concluding passage from Stephen Hawking's *A Brief History of Time*, where Hawking confidently asserts that a Grand Unified Theory, as a complete theory that would be able to explain everything about the universe – including why it exists – would be discovered within the competence of physics, and would as such be the same as knowing the mind of God (cf. Hawking 1990: 175). Although Davies borrows the phrase 'the mind of God' from Hawking, he eventually fundamentally disagrees with him. For Davies there will always be the 'mystery at the end of the universe' (1992: 223ff.), and thus he concedes that the nature of human rationality as well as of the laws of nature are such that they alone can never answer the ultimate questions of existence.

What is astounding, however, is to what a great extent our world is truly rational, i.e., in conformity with human reason. For Davies our human intelligence clearly resonates with the remarkable intelligibility of our world, and the human mind is capable of grasping the complex natural laws upon which the universe runs. That human rationality resonates so well with the laws of nature that it is capable of discovering the mathematical principles of these laws leads Davies to the conclusion that:

> . . . the existence of conscious organisms is a *fundamental* feature of the universe. We have been written into the laws of nature in a deep and, I believe, meaningful way (1992: 21).

For Paul Davies our own species, *Homo sapiens*, thus carries the spark of rationality that provides the key to understanding our universe, and in this sense we are truly meant to be here (1992: 232). Davies very specifically does not subscribe to a conventional religion but he nevertheless explicitly wants to deny that the universe is a purposeless accident. And it is at precisely this point that he emphasizes that mind, or our conscious awareness of the world, is not at all a meaningless and incidental quirk of nature, but is rather a fundamental facet of reality (cf. 1992: 26). This does not mean, in any simplistic way, that we humans are the purpose for which the universe exists. It does mean, however, that we human beings are built into the scheme of things in a very basic way.

As we will see later, it is exactly this crucially important point that is picked up today by current trends in evolutionary epistemology as philosophers and theologians probe the origins and limitations of human rationality in a renewed quest for a comprehensive view of human knowledge. For Davies even the most basic aspects of human thought must ultimately refer back to observations of the physical world. Even those concepts that are most deeply etched in our psyche – such as 'common sense' and 'human rationality' – are those that are genetically programmed at a very deep level in our brains (cf. 1992: 23). Our mental processes, therefore, have evolved as they have precisely because they reflect something of the nature of the physical world we inhabit. Davies thus rejects explanations which would argue that the universe came into existence accidentally and that the human mind is a product of blind chance. Although evolution can explain why we have, for instance, developed reflexes to dodge falling rocks, it cannot explain why we can understand the laws which govern falling bodies, why these laws are there, and why we have the ability to discover them mathematically. Our human brains therefore are indeed the product of physical processes, but for Davies they can never be explained by those processes alone (cf. 1992: 171). The laws of nature, our ability to unlock mathematically the secrets of the deeper regularities they point to, and the ultimate 'why' questions that we ask as a result of all of this, point to the deeper mystery of the universe of which we and our rational abilities are an integral part.

And it is this rational ability, this process of human reasoning, that Paul Davies wants to take as far as it will go, but it is also this very same process of human reasoning that is ultimately revealed as limited and unable to provide us with answers to the ultimate 'why' – questions. And Davies is right: we are barred from ultimate explanations by the very rules of reasoning that prompt us to seek such an explanation in the first place (cf. 1992: 231). From this it does become clear that, in Davies' mind, concepts like 'reasonable' and 'rational' are always narrowly identified with natural science and natural scientific knowledge. But it is the more important notion of the limits of scientific rationality that finally pushed Davies to argue for a different concept of 'understanding', and for a mystical path as a way to such an understanding (cf. 1992: 232).

It is indeed fascinating to see, precisely through the fact that the rational nature of our universe is reflected in its basic mathematical structure, that Davies ultimately comes to the point where he has to acknowledge the limits of this reasonableness. The very limitations of mathematics itself was decisively revealed by Gödel in his famous argument that the very axioms upon which mathematics is constructed cannot be proved true or false by the same mathematics (cf. 1992: 101ff., 255). There therefore exist unprovable truths, undecidable assumptions and propositions that cannot be proved to be true. Mathematical statements therefore exist for which no systematic procedure could determine whether they really are true or false. And if this is true for mathematical reasoning – for Davies the apex of human rationality – then surely it is true for all other forms of rational human reasoning too.

Davies' approach to the problems that surface at the disciplinary boundaries of contemporary cosmology certainly is a huge step forward from the resolutely reductionist program that Stephen Hawking left us with. In a necessary universe that 'just is', our universe could never be anything other than what it already is, and it would not need any further explanation of the ground of its existence, for its very existence would be the reason for its being, and nothing more. Such was the basis on which Hawking's Theory of Everything was pursued, but Davies has made us aware of the fact that exactly this kind of search for a closed and logical scheme, which provides a complete and self-consistent explanation for everything, is doomed to failure (cf. 1992: 226). In his argument for a contingent universe, Davies sides with Ian Barbour and finds convincing arguments for this notion in the fact that the laws of physics seem contingent, the initial conditions of the universe could have been different, there is fundamental indeterminism in nature, and of course the universe exists – there is indeed something rather than nothing (cf. 1992: 169ff.). What this leaves us with is either to accept this universe, and our good luck to be part of it, as a brute fact, or to go ahead and admit that both we and our universe are meant to exist in ways which science just cannot explain (cf. Park 1994: 8f.).

Davies' next step is quite remarkable and perfectly in line with some of our most important contemporary theories of rationality: for this kind of all-important decision, Davies again does not appeal narrowly to science, or to scientific rationality, but rather to personal judgment: 'In the end, Occam's razor compels me to put my money on design, but, as always in matters of metaphysics, the decision is largely a matter of taste rather than scientific judgment' (1992: 220). Exactly by appealing to the all-important skill of responsible, personal judgment in his choice for an ordered, purposeful cosmos that ultimately points to 'a mystery at the end of the universe', Davies significantly broadens the scope of human rationality in ways that could deeply affect and enrich natural scientific rationality too (cf. J.W. van Huyssteen 1998b).

Davies' well-known statement that 'there will always be mystery at the end of the universe' (1992: 225) indeed opens up the way for richer and more comprehensive ways of understanding our world, and, in his particular case, for other forms of understanding – especially mysticism – by means of which we may be enabled finally to address the ultimate questions of our existence. Those of us who live on the risky boundaries of interdisciplinary reflection can only applaud Davies' much more nuanced progress from a narrow focus on (only) natural scientific rationality, to other and broader forms of rational understanding. Of course, just the mere choice for mystical ways of understanding is ultimately still not really satisfactory. Somehow it still comes across as seriously reductionistic to allow only for mysticism as another form of understanding *vis à vis* natural science: theology too is a distinct form of human knowledge, i.e., a distinct form of rational reflection on religious experience that not only could be markedly different from mysticism, but which could in fact, as a reasoning strategy, share important overlaps with the rationality of the natural sciences. Davies is therefore right in arguing that the answers to our ultimate questions lie beyond the scope of empirical science. The choice for the mystical path may indeed open up alternative ways of understanding here, but actually so does the choice for theology as a systematic reflection on religious experience. Rightly understood, the rationality of theology in no way bypasses human reason: it may indeed transcend in scope the limits of a strictly natural scientific rationality, but it certainly shares with the sciences the quest for intelligibility and ultimate meaning.

Ironically, then, Paul Davies' rigorous investigation of the limits of scientific rationality is rewarding to those of us who are not committed only to natural scientific ways of understanding the world. Davies, as we saw, wants to suggest mysticism as a possible way to gain ultimate knowledge of the world. Ultimately, however, we are left unclear as to what exactly he might mean by this, even though he supplies us with various examples of mystical experiences among physicists. Davies leaves open the question as to what role mysticism might actually play in any such ultimate quest. More importantly, though, Davies essentially by-passes the fact that mysticism has been a crucially important aspect of various religions. In fact, in his descriptions of the role of mystical events in physicists' lives, he focuses only on the remarkable phenomenon of creative insight-experiences, and never on the religious implications, or on the specific religious content that could have been qualified and strengthened by these mystical experiences (cf. H.F. van Huyssteen 1996: 1ff.). We are left with the distinct impression that what Davies really wants is a mystical experience that really is devoid of specific religious content.

Although Paul Davies' broadening of scientific rationality should be welcomed since it gets him far beyond Hawking's rigid scientism, the rich and complex history of mysticism is left unexplored in Davies' work and therefore still leaves open the question of how science should relate to religion. Hawking, of course, would dispute even the notion of ultimate questions about an ultimate reality, since the laws of nature, revealed through our scientific observation of it, are for him the only reality. Davies does, however, give us an all-important key in acknowledging so openly the limits of natural scientific rationality, even as he sees mystical thought as something that lies at the opposite extreme of rational thought, which for him still is the basis of the scientific method (cf. Davies 1992: 226).

Conclusion

Our conversation with Stephen Hawking and Paul Davies has revealed how important it is for theologians to engage in the work of contemporary cosmologists, but also how much theology has to learn from cosmology, even as it critically engages with the quasi-theologies or metaphysics of contemporary scientists. This critically important conversation will also liberate theology from naively ignoring, or uncritically assessing, contemporary cosmological challenges.

We should therefore be very open to the fact that science can, and should, directly influence theology, and this influence happens when the results of scientific investigation, or the methodologies of science directly impact theology. The natural sciences also have a direct impact on theology through new images, perspectives, symbols, and stories. As far as cosmology and its impact on theology goes, theology has to take very seriously the general conclusions and findings of contemporary cosmology – that is, that the universe is as large and as old as it is, that this universe is evolving, that all that is within it has had a common physical origin in time, and that all it contains is in principle explicable by the natural sciences (cf. Stoeger 1988: 239). The cosmologist, however, should be aware of the fact that there are limits to scientific explanations in cosmology, and that therefore empirical justification or verification is in principle always limited: a fact that very closely relates to the interdisciplinary nature of cosmology, as we saw earlier. There are indeed certain things about the universe that we will most probably never know for sure, and certain questions about physical reality which cosmology will never be able to address.

When we become aware of the fallibilist nature of all

human knowledge – also scientific knowledge – it also becomes reasonable to accept the fact that science cannot be expected any more ever to grant us a 'theory of everything' in the true, comprehensive sense of the word. Scientific inquiry certainly provides us with excellent accounts of certain important aspects of reality: it cannot, however, provide us with an account of every aspect of reality. To Stephen Hawking's claim that a complete set of scientific laws would reveal to us the 'mind of God', we should answer that the most these laws could reveal for the Christian believer will be God's intentions for the very small and the very large (cf. Anderson 1995: 22). Precisely because of the limitations of natural scientific rationality, even the laws of nature should not be treated prescriptively as revealing the regularities and relationships of reality in itself, but as descriptively pointing to these regularities in terms of detailed descriptions or models that we make of them and to which we then refer as the 'laws of nature' (cf. Stoeger 1988: 11f.). That is why John Horgan is not just wrong, but almost absurd when he argues (cf. 1996) that we are close to reaching the end of science, because the laws of nature that we have determined will soon explain all (cf. H.F. van Huyssteen 1996: 9).

Scientific laws, therefore, do not determine, nor do they reveal, God's intentions for human beings. In order to know what God wants for us as human beings, we must find a different way of structuring and organizing our knowledge of reality: and this redescription is the task of theology (cf. Gregersen 1994: 12ff.; also Anderson 1995: 22). Moreover, as a result of the clear limitations of scientific rationality, there will most probably always be explanatory gaps in any scientific account of the evolutionary development of the universe. Any 'God of the gaps' form of explanation should, however, always be avoided and wherever gaps in our understanding occur within a scientific context, they should be left for the scientific disciplines themselves to fill (cf. Stoeger 1988: 239). These gaps inevitably end up being bridged by science itself, because at its own level science is capable of providing adequate and complete explanations.

But how about the very obvious question: did God then create the universe through the Big Bang? Or as Ted Peters put it, did God start the Big Bang, and light the fuse of the cosmic dynamite (cf. 1989: 58f.)? We should be extremely careful in establishing a too easy parallel, or consonance, between 'the beginning of time' in the Big Bang and 'the beginning of time' in the Christian doctrine of creation. It seems to be very unlikely that cosmology as a science will be able to unveil a point of absolute beginning, before which nothing existed, before which time of any sort was not, which would as such somehow already require the direct influence of God (cf. Stoeger 1988: 240). The fact that cosmology might not be able to explain such an event completely does not mean it might not have occurred. It does, however, mean that cosmology is not able to discover it as a religious event of immense theological importance. The limits of scientific rationality therefore indeed seem to point beyond that rationality to a deeper religious mystery. It is exactly the epistemic limitations of natural scientific reflection, as well as the limitations of theological reflection, which should find practical acknowledgment in our ongoing interdisciplinary conversation.

But in the interdisciplinary conversation between theology and cosmology we should quickly learn to avoid epistemological short cuts, and we need to be alert to the following: it would be possible to say, theologically, that if our universe had a beginning in time through the unique act of a creator, then from this theological point of view it would look something like the Big Bang cosmologists are talking about. What one cannot say is that the doctrine of creation 'supports' the Big Bang model, or that the Big Bang 'supports' the Christian doctrine of creation (cf. McMullin 1981: 39). As Christians we should therefore take very seriously the theories of physics and cosmology: not to exploit or to try to change them, but to try to find interpretations that would suggest some form of complementary consonance with the Christian viewpoint. Theology cannot, therefore, ever claim to be capable of scientific theory-appraisal, but should rather be seen as one (important) voice in the constructing of broader and interdisciplinary world-views. The Christian can never separate her or his science from her or his theology, but she or he should also learn to distrust epistemological short cuts from the one to the other. One way to do this would be to find a comprehensive model that would yield the kind of fine-tuned epistemological consonance we need for a true interdisciplinary 'dance' or 'duet'.

Also, instead of asking whether God created our universe through the Big Bang, we should rather ask why Christians hold to the belief commitments they have about creation. For instance, to the heart of the Christian faith commitment belongs the strong conviction that, if God really is God, then God must be responsible for all that is. This kind of 'Creator concept' is implied by the heart of the Christian Gospel: only a God that is 'almighty', i.e., a God who can create something out of nothing (*ex nihilo*), will be able to conquer death through the resurrection of Christ. For this kind of deep, religious convictions we do indeed need the enduring and exciting tradition of the biblical narrative in Genesis 1 and 2.

Seen in this broader interdisciplinary context, the biblical creation story still has profound religious meaning, a meaning that is not affected by today's emerging cosmological theories and models, because a myth is never just true or false, but is either living or dead (cf. Peters 1989: 58f.). Theology and science can thus, independently, make statements about the same world, and some of the same aspects of our universe (its origin, dynamic character, evolution, its amazing order, its future, etc.) are therefore indeed subject to both scientific interpretation and theological redescription. These descriptions, however, must be epistemologically clarified as to their often very different epistemic focus and explanatory status; only then will they fit together without contradictions.

Thus are revealed some of the philosophical and epistemological complexities involved in trying to relate theology and science today. We now also know that genuine conflicts between science and theology are exceedingly difficult to detect and specify accurately. In retrospect many of these serious clashes turn out to be not between religion and science, but between incompatible, even incommensurable world views or philosophies (cf. Lash 1985: 277). The current focus on the complex but challenging relationship between theology and cosmology suggests, however, a fall from epistemological innocence regarding this fascinating issue. For the philosophical theologian this presents a challenge to his or her personal commitments and beliefs: a challenge that also implies a quest for a plausible model of theological contextuality, because it thrusts to the front questions about the status of religious claims to knowledge, and about the rationality of belief in God.

Ultimately, what is at stake, at least for theology in the

current theology and science dialogue, is whether or not it would be possible plausibly to revise the belief that God works out God's purposes in and through the processes of the natural world. The kind of comprehensive epistemology that would yield this kind of stunning interdisciplinary result would at the same time yield a truly sacramental theology: a vision in which the creative and evolutionary processes visible to the sciences are revealed as truly non-deterministic and genuinely open to creative novelty, but which at the same time provides the very locus of God's continuous activity. But this kind of creative epistemological space for a dialogue between theology and the sciences would only be truly inter-disciplinary if it eventually also included disciplines such as psychology, sociology and anthropology, which deal with precisely those properties which have arisen in our own species, *Homo sapiens,* as genuine emergent properties of the universe. For it may be precisely these emergent properties, with their amazing sacramental potential, that ultimately and decisively point us to God (cf. Knight 1995: 44). It is to these issues that we now turn in the final two chapters.

3

Religion and Knowledge

Does Evolution hold the Key?

Introduction

Already in our discussion of the relationship between theology and cosmology, it became abundantly clear that what is at stake in this complex affair is basically the nature and origin of human knowledge. The real question indeed seems to be whether such extremely diverse forms of human knowledge, like theology and science, could actually be brought into conversation with one another in spite of the radical fragmentation of knowledge effected by some forms of sceptical postmodernism. We also saw, however, that it would be almost impossible to be content with a plurality of different, fragmented and unrelated forms of knowledge if these in fact claim, in one way or another, to be knowledge of the same world.

But is there a way towards a comprehensive form of human knowledge which would not be vulnerable to the postmodern disillusionment with all totalizing and universalizing forms of knowledge, and which might actually point to a comprehensive epistemology that would not only make possible, but actually enhance our interdisciplinary reflection? An important pointer towards such a postfoundationalist view was already found in the fact that theology and cosmology, although widely diverse as reasoning strategies, are both essentially interdisciplinary in nature and as such share deeply in the quest for a more comprehensive and inter-related knowledge of the origin, the meaning and the destiny of our universe. We also saw that contemporary cosmology explicitly argues for treating the observable universe as a single object, which would imply that in some way or other the universe must have at least some form of intelligibility as a single object of study. This almost necessarily presupposes and implies a kind of comprehensive epistemology that would reflect precisely the interdisciplinary nature of this mode of knowledge.

Not only in cosmology, but also in evolutionary epistemology, however, there are strong arguments today for the emergence of exactly such a comprehensive view of human knowledge. As will become clear later, evolutionary episte-mology will reveal a quite remarkable ability to facilitate and embrace this quest for a comprehensive account of human knowledge, a quest already so alive and well in theology and cosmology today. However, other deeper connections between cosmology and theology have also become clear. In the previous chapter the important question 'How can we think of the universe, the cosmos, as God's creation?' has already revealed to us one crucially important perspective: our universe essentially is an evolving universe. From the standpoint of contemporary science, the whole history of the universe is in fact a history of evolution. On our planet, that process of evolution has continued, as simple atoms of carbon, hydrogen, oxygen and other elements built up and developed into the millions of life-forms that now exist on earth. That such a process has taken place is one of the foundations of contemporary modern science. In fact, the idea of evolution itself has now become a theory with tremendous explanatory force, a theory that explains many otherwise puzzling features of our world in a very elegant way (cf. Ward 1996: 61).

As in the case of cosmology and theology, biology and theology are obviously based on modes of knowledge, reasoning strategies and methodologies that are radically different almost to the extreme. They do, however, share one focal interest, i.e., an interest in what we may call life processes: obviously, the discovery of fundamental life processes and their structure and manifestations is the explicit task of biology (cf. Gregersen 1994: 124). Exactly these life processes, at least in a broader sense, fall under the broad, interdisciplinary scope of theology too, because the Judeo-Christian belief in 'creation' traditionally brings into focus the origin of life itself. As theology's ongoing interdisciplinary conversation with philosophy and cosmology has shown, theological reflection is deeply concerned with some of life's most profound and ultimate questions. Exactly for these reasons Niels Gregersen has persuasively argued that theology is in fact so much more than the mere interpretation of texts: it is, in fact, concerned with the interpretation of existence, and as such the theological world view by definition implies a radical redescription of the world from an informed Christian point of view (cf. Gregersen 1994: 125f.). But, we may ask, if the theory of evolution has been so extraordinarily successful in explaining life processes, and even the origin of life on our planet, does this necessarily mean that the theory of evolution and Christian doctrines of 'creation' and 'providence' are for ever going to be on a collision course with one another?

The thesis of this chapter will be exactly the opposite: I

believe that a theological redescription of the process of evolution, and a creative complementary integration of the results of contemporary evolutionary biology, could be eminently rational and could offer a persuasive alternative to resolutely scientistic or radically naturalistic readings of the same material. I therefore accept the theory of evolution as one of the major insights of contemporary science. I also believe that a responsible theological redescription of these issues should make it clear why the idea of God, and of God's presence in this universe, can move us beyond disputes like whether evolution operates through blind chance or providence, whether naturalism or supernaturalism are the only options open to Christian believers, and whether we should, therefore, feel forced to choose between these two narrow options as the only available constructs for explaining the origin and evolution of life on our planet. I therefore believe that evolution, rightly understood, can enrich our religious faith considerably, and may actually set the stage for a friendly and rewarding 'duet' between religion and science.

By now we should know, however, that there are no easy short cuts from historical conflicts to friendly conversation between these two dominant forces in our culture. The complexity of the historical relationship between theology and evolution becomes clearer if we take a cue from postmodern philosophy of science and take seriously some of its challenges to scientific reflection. As we saw earlier in Chapter 1, the most typical of these challenges is the radical call for contextual or local science and for a new focus on the social and historical embeddedness of the individual scientist. To do this adequately we would have to go back to the 'source' and learn from Charles Darwin's own radical embeddedness in Victorian culture and the natural theology of the time. In fact, the case of Charles Darwin can be an excellent example not only for discussing epistemic issues like the goals and methods of science, the problems of the limits of rationality and progress in science, and the social structure of science, but also for asking what the relationship of the individual scientist would be to the collective rationality of the reigning scientific community (cf. Kitcher 1993: 10f.). These are some of the reasons why in this context we can – albeit only briefly – touch upon the important question as to why Darwin's science and his attitude to the Christian faith are still important for all our attempts to relate theology constructively to the theory of evolution. By looking at what Darwin himself thought of the religious implications of his work, and at the ways his science was indebted to theology, it will indeed become possible to trace the complex interaction between Darwin's growing confidence in his theory of evolution by natural selection, and his increasing doubts about religious belief in the second half of his life (cf. Durant 1985).

A (very) dangerous duet?

The publication of Charles Darwin's *On the Origin of Species* in 1859 in many ways was the most important event in the ongoing history of ideas of our culture and as such represents an intellectual revolution that continues to affect many areas of thought today. The theory of evolution by natural selection has possibly changed our views of nature, of God, and of God's relation to nature, more than any other theory in the history of human thought. Two very basic ideas have always been central to Darwin's theory of evolution by natural selection: first, in every population there are small random variations which can be inherited; second, in the struggle for survival some of these variations manage a slight competitive advantage, which over many generations leads to the natural selection of those characteristics that ultimately contributed to survival (cf. Barbour 1997: 221). For Darwin it was through such a process of natural selection that new species finally came into existence. The direct result of these now famous views understandably saw science as demythologizing our world and as such in direct conflict with religion. The traditional picture of a universe where everything revolves around the drama of human life and death was now indeed and successfully replaced with a far bleaker picture of the universe as completely devoid of centre, and of human purpose. John Durant puts this well: first in cosmology, with Galileo, then in biology, with Darwin, and finally in psychology, with Freud, we are confronted with the fact that we are mere fragments in a world that appears to be neither about us nor for us (cf. Durant 1985: 9). This was in stark opposition to earlier views which still assumed that the forms of all living things were fixed when they were created as part of an unchanging and ordered universe. On the evolutionary view, however, all nature is dynamic, changing and fundamentally historical in character. Previously, humanity was sharply distinguished from the rest of nature, but since Darwin, humanity has been understood to be part of nature, the product of a common evolutionary heritage (cf. Barbour 1997: 221).

Darwin's theory of evolution by natural selection therefore clearly states that living beings reproduce themselves with very slight variations over many generations, and are engaged in an ongoing struggle for life while competing with other living beings and with the forces of nature. This then was

Darwin's ingenious answer to the 'mystery of mysteries', the problem of identifying those processes driving the development and succession of organisms in such a way that some species had become extinct, while the earth's fauna is somehow constantly renewed. At the heart of Darwin's theory of evolution by natural selection then was also an answer to the burning question why similar species would have important differences if they lived in quite similar environmental conditions. Darwin's radically new idea rested on four fundamental claims, which in the *Origin of Species* ultimately unfolded in five important principles (cf. Kitcher 1993: 19f.):

(i) At any stage in the history of a species, there will always be variation among different members of the species (the principle of variation);

(ii) At any stage in the history of a species, more members are born that can survive to reproduce (the principle of the struggle for existence);

(iii) At any stage in the history of a species, some of the variation among members of the species is variation with respect to properties that affect the ability to survive and reproduce: some members of a species therefore have characteristics that help them survive and reproduce (the principle of variation in fitness);

(iv) Heritability is the norm, and most properties of an organism or member of a species are inherited by its descendants (the principle of inheritance);

These four principles converge in one final argument:

(v) Typically the history of a species will show the modification of that species in the direction of those characteristics which help their bearers to survive and reproduce; and these characteristics are then likely to become more prevalent in successive generations of the species (the principle of natural selection).

Darwin therefore attempted to show that it is indeed possible to modify organisms extensively through a process of natural selection, and in this sense Darwin himself would see *The Origin of Species* as one long argument for evolution by natural selection (cf. Kitcher 1993: 26). This would obviously, and importantly, imply that all organisms now classified as separate species are in fact related by descent from a common ancestor. Exactly the comprehensive scope of this groundbreaking evolutionary idea would of course directly challenge traditional Christian faith: first, as a challenge to literalist readings of the Bible, since the slow, gradual process of evolution can in no way be easily reconciled with a divine creation in seven days, as reported in the first chapter of Genesis; second, as a direct challenge to human dignity: traditionally Christians would view human beings as fundamentally different from other creatures because of their immortal souls, because they were created 'in the image of God', and because of the unique distinctiveness of human rationality; third, as a direct challenge to design and divine purpose, because Darwin successfully showed that adaptation could be accounted for by an impersonal process of variation and natural selection (cf. Barbour 1997: 222f.). Ultimately, as we will see, the theory of evolution by natural selection would also explode any simplistic and easy distinctions between what is 'natural' and what is 'supernatural', and as such it would directly challenge Christian notions of God.

Religion and Knowledge

Charles Darwin, as is well known, did not of course invent the idea of evolution, even if he has been the most influential exponent of the idea, and it is at this point that the social-historical embeddedness of Darwin's ideas gains particular importance for relating evolution to Christian faith and theology today. Darwin's intellectual growth and maturity obviously did not happen in a vacuum, but rather Darwin's ideas originated in nineteenth-century Great Britain where science was not so much opposed to, or in conflict with, religion and theology, but rather was done within the larger context of religious belief. This fact is important for the understanding and assessment of the relationship between Darwinism and religious belief and provides us with a special perspective for evaluating the strong conflict that would later erupt between natural selection and natural theology. During the first half of the nineteenth century the debate about natural history was indeed part of a larger debate about the interrelationship between God, nature, human nature and society, and natural theology was central to the work of English naturalists in the nineteenth century, of whom William Paley – of 'watchmaker God' fame – was arguably the most famous example (cf. Durant 1985: 13f.).

Paley's most basic theological conviction that nature, and also human nature, exemplified God's wisdom, design, providence, justice and benevolence as the Creator of God's fortunate people, was rudely shattered with the anonymous publication in 1844 of the infamous *Vestiges of the Natural History of Creation*. In this book the Edinburgh publisher Robert Chambers, later revealed as the mysterious author, argued the case for a natural law of development governing the history of life, a law which should be extended to include the physical, mental and moral qualities of humankind. John

Durant has argued persuasively that the controversy that accompanied the publication of the *Vestiges* marked the critical point in Victorian debates about science and religious belief, a point that also reveals to us a world view on the point of collapse (cf. Durant 1985: 15f.). Chambers' conviction that God's revelation should be seen as a system based on law, and not as a system independent of the Deity, was in fact a natural theological attempt to show how God works through the laws of nature. His deterministic appeal to providence, however, created great controversy, superseded later only by Darwin's very different and much more careful, and successful, theory of evolution by natural selection.

In the light of these ongoing debates in the early and mid-nineteenth century, John Durant is certainly correct in calling Darwin's 1859 publication of *The Origin of Species* the last great work of Victorian natural theology. This statement also has to be qualified, however: the *Origin* also is the first, and greatest, work of Victorian evolutionary naturalism (cf. Durant 1985: 16). In order to understand Charles Darwin's work properly, therefore, it is important to know that he was trained in the tradition of English natural theology, that the problems with which he dealt were those of English natural theology, and that the audience at which he aimed *The Origin of Species* consisted overwhelmingly of English natural theologians. This famous book is therefore totally embedded in the paradigm and conventions of English natural theology. This becomes strikingly clear when we listen to Darwin's own words in the final pages of *The Origin of Species*:

> Authors of the highest eminence seem to be fully satisfied with the view that each species has been independently

created. To my mind it accords better with what we know of the laws impressed on matter by the Creator, that the production and extinction of the past and present inhabitants of the world should have been due to secondary causes, like those determining the birth and death of the individual . . . Judging from the past, we may safely infer that not one living species will transmit its unaltered likeness to a distant futurity (Darwin 1985: 458f.).

The natural secondary causes that Darwin invokes here are of course the now well-known elements of variation, overproduction, struggle for existence and natural selection. What is often overlooked, however, is that Darwin at this stage in his life explicitly invited his readers to see these causes as the means adopted by the Creator to populate the earth (cf. also Durant 1985: 17). Darwin's views on religion and religious faith became increasingly ambiguous, however, as he grew older. The mere fact that Darwinism initially was developed within the tradition of English natural theology already raises important questions regarding the nature of Darwin's personal views on religion. Both John Brooke (1985) and John Durant (1985) have carefully analysed both what Darwin himself thought of the religious implications of his work and the ways Darwin's science was indebted to his theology, while at the same time tracing the complex interaction between Darwin's growing confidence in his evolutionary theory and his increasing doubts about religious belief in the second half of his life.

Darwin himself was reluctant even to discuss his own gradual loss of faith, possibly out of respect for his wife Emma's deep personal faith. He did, however, acknowledge that his own personal beliefs often fluctuated, and later in life he would follow his friend Huxley and call himself an 'agnostic'. Darwin did, however, always agonize about what he was supposed to say in public and wondered if it would be 'gentlemanly' to confess one's religious doubts if by so doing one risked hurting the feelings of others (cf. Brooke 1985: 40f.). Any statement of Darwin about religion and religious faith therefore has to be interpreted with these kind of dilemmas in mind. This is especially true when we attempt today to understand what Darwin thought about God. In spite of extreme fluctuations when it came to religious faith, Darwin never saw himself as an atheist, at least not in the sense of denying the existence of God: something the Princeton theologian Charles Hodge would understand very well, as we will soon see, in spite of his severe criticism of Darwinism soon after the publication of *The Origin of Species*. John Brooke has therefore persuasively argued that Charles Darwin seems to have retained the 'inward conviction' that the universe as a whole could not have been the product of blind chance only. Darwin certainly, however, later became agnostic about the importance that should be attached to this conviction (cf. Brooke 1985: 42).

That Darwin's ever more confident vision of biological adaptation as an evolving process was in direct antithesis to the argument from design in natural theology is certainly undeniable. But that Darwin's theory of natural selection was so embedded in the broader context of English natural theology, and that his own views of God and God's action in the world always were rather ambiguous, should prevent us from too easily reducing the relationship of Darwin's theory of evolution to natural theology to the conventional antithesis or conflict between religion and science. This is true even if Darwin was profoundly unmoved by any 'transcendental interpretation of bones' and most certainly rejected any design arguments which would find a divine blueprint for God's creation in the structure of the animal world. Exactly on this point John Brooke argues beautifully that Darwin genuinely believed that the philosophy of nature which he was discovering pointed to a new grandeur of the deity (cf. Brooke 1985: 45f.). The belief that the Creator creates through the laws of nature was therefore firmly embedded in Darwin's mind. This shines through in the famous final sentence of the very last page of *The Origin of Species*:

> There is a grandeur in this view of life, with its several powers, having been originally breathed into a few forms or into one; and that, whilst this planet has gone cycling on according to the fixed law of gravity, from so simple a beginning endless forms most beautiful and most wonderful have been, and are being, evolved (Darwin 1985: 459f.).

In retrospect the *Origin* certainly represents a secularizing trend in mid-Victorian natural theology, since here the revelation of God in the works of nature came to be seen as having been written exclusively in the language of the laws of nature (cf. Durant 1985: 17). It could also certainly be argued that, although his science initially was deeply influenced by this kind of natural theology, Darwin did become more and more resolutely naturalist and ultimately lost conviction in a providentially designed system, thereby taking the theology out of the science. To the end, however, the relationship between Darwin's science and his loss of religious conviction was complex and problematical. One thing remains certain, however: precisely by finding it impossible, if not offensive (cf. Brooke 1985: 67), to understand particular events in providentialist terms, Darwin raised enduring questions for Christian theology.

Right from the beginning these questions revealed serious concern from different and opposing sides about the ideological dimension of the debates about the origin of life. At the heart of the controversies about the theory of evolution there was a moral concern that was there right from the beginning: John Durant relates how on Christmas Eve in 1859, Darwin's old friend and geology teacher, Adam Sedgwick, wrote to his former pupil that he had read the *Origin* 'with more pain than pleasure'. Just a month before that Darwin's close friend and defender, Thomas Huxley, had written that in writing the *Origin* Darwin had 'earned the lasting gratitude of all thoughtful men'. Sedgwick believed that Darwin had made a great mistake, and that Darwinism threatened to degrade the human race by disrupting the intimate connections between science and theology. Huxley, however, was convinced of a great and exciting advance in science and believed that Darwin's work marked a long-awaited break between science and theology: this was no tragedy, but rather a triumph of the free spirit of rational and scientific inquiry. It is clear why the views of Sedgwick and Huxley would in time come to symbolize much in the debates that were to follow: all were united, at least, in their conviction that far more was at stake in the *Origin* than the title of the book appeared to suggest (cf. Durant 1985: 3f.).

An (all too) friendly duel?

To get an adequate grasp of what was at stake for theology, but especially for the notion of God, in the ongoing dialogue with evolution, it will be important and helpful to take a brief look at one of the earliest and most important North American responses to Darwin, that of Charles Hodge of Princeton Theological Seminary. Princeton holds a special place in the early Darwinian controversies, and certainly not only in the United States of America. The intellectual culture which flourished at the Seminary and at the University (then the College) during much of the nineteenth century combined Scottish common sense realism and orthodox Reformed theology. Philosophically there may be good reasons for seeing the 'Princeton paradigm' (cf. Stewart 1995) as an historically extinct position, but theologically the Old Princetonians at both institutions developed – also in their ongoing conversation with one another – a powerful model for relating theology to science, aspects of which are still challenging for us today. This is especially true of the 'theology of nature' which was to mediate the relationship between theology and science and which certainly was superior to the kind of natural theology Charles Darwin was rebelling against and finally completely rejected (cf.Burnett 1994: 2). The challenge presented by Darwinism certainly forced the scholars of Old Princeton to express their understanding of 'theology and science issues' more explicitly than ever before.

Any attempt to understand Charles Hodge on this point would therefore have to be preceded by asking: what exactly was this Princeton 'theology of nature' and its supporting epistemological sub-structure? In many ways Hodge was an entirely conventional theologian of Presbyterian orthodoxy, subscribing to consistently conservative positions whenever confessional guidelines made them possible to identify (cf. Burnett 1994: 10). At the same time, however, his activities as a prolific writer and reviewer of books and articles on a wide range of issues reveal him as a quite remarkable interdisciplinary thinker, and kept him in genuine dialogue with other views and disciplines. At the heart of this – what today we would call a fundamentally interdisciplinary approach – was Hodge's definition of theology as a 'science', with a deliberate and consistent analogy to the methodology and rationality of the natural sciences. As an amateur scientist Hodge was also sensitive to the increasing cultural authority accorded to science. And although today we may find it strange that anyone could even consider the idea that theological 'facts' may be epistemically on a par with scientific 'facts', I will argue that Hodge's basic conviction, that scientific and theological world views should not be mutually exclusive because of some basic 'unity of truth', is – complete with postmodern garb – again the centre and focus of much of our contemporary interdisciplinary discussion and our ongoing quest for a comprehensive view of human knowledge.

Therefore, if Hodge can today with good reasons be blamed for failing to appropriate the currents of modern thought (Stewart 1995: 1), he – at least theologically – directly anticipated much of the discussions about the epistemological ramifications of the demise of modernity in our times: in philosophical (or interdisciplinary) theology, it is precisely the problem of 'design' and the quest for a 'unity of truth' (today more fallibilistically rephrased as the quest for comprehensive knowledge, and the postfoundationalist revisioning of the shared resources of human rationality) that still are at the heart of our discussions in philosophical theology today. Hodge's refusal to succumb to the modernist dilemma of rigorously opposing objective, scientific knowledge to subjective/irrational religious/theological opinion was indeed his (intuitive) way of dealing with some of the most problematical trends in modern thought, and he did it by just bluntly refusing to buy into this dilemma.

Stewart is therefore correct in arguing that Charles Hodge needs to be evaluated on his own terms and placed at the centre of those lively discourses that flourished in the mid-nineteenth century between Reformed thought and (American) culture. In this sense it would indeed be fruitful to look at Hodge as, first of all, a theologian of culture (cf. Stewart 1995: 2) and as such to find his place in the history of theological ideas of his times. Stewart has argued that Hodge's oeuvre can only be adequately appreciated if seen through the way Hodge appropriated the particular American culture of the day by way of the so-called 'Princeton paradigm'. For Stewart this antebellum Princeton paradigm mixed three interactive ingredients: first, an epistemological grounding in Scottish common sense realism; second, a commitment to what is called a 'doxological science' that assumed no insurmountable demarcation between science and religion; and, third, a growing notion that theology itself should be understood and pursued as a science (cf. Stewart 1995: 22f.). The 'Princeton paradigm' certainly included the traditions of Scottish common sense philosophy, but it also included a thoroughly popularized argument from design, which seemingly served to cement a strong methodological parallel between theology and science. These themes very much served as 'epistemological foundations' for Charles Hodge's theology.

In retrospect, and from a contemporary history of ideas point of view, only the first element of this paradigm, i.e., Hodge's intellectual embeddedness in Scottish common sense realism, can today clearly be identified as an historically extinct position. However, this cultural embeddedness in his version of Scottish realism can never be such a liability that it would detract from his enduring contributions to the other dimensions of the Princeton paradigm. Certainly no one today sees theology as a 'doxological science' any more, but the constructive aspect of the postmodern challenge of our times has certainly revived the important issue of interdisciplinary reflection and is now directly opposing any rigid demarcation between religion/theology and science. Hodge's strong conviction that theology somehow qualifies as rational reflection, and his resulting assumption that there could be no insurmountable demarcation between theology and science, looked at from a history-of-ideas point of view, certainly directly anticipates some of today's hotly-debated epistemological challenges to the ongoing dialogue between theology and science. These can be identified as follows: first, the collapse of rigid, modernist disciplinary distinctions into a more interdisciplinary intellectual space, where, second, traditional epistemic boundaries and disciplinary distinctions are blurred precisely because the same kind of interpretative procedures are at work in all our diverse reasoning strategies, and, third, through the creative fusion of hermeneutics and epistemology, reasoning strategies as distinctive and different as theology and the sciences may be revealed actually both to share the rich resources of human rationality. Admittedly the contemporary debates about the mutual sharing of the resources of human rationality are very far removed from a Hodgean quest for truth where both the 'facts of nature' and the 'facts of the Bible' shared a revelatory status (cf. Stewart 1995: 26f.). Despite these contextual and cultural trappings, however, the contemporary postfoundationalist attempt to clear a safe epistemological space for a conversation between a truly public theology and the sciences today revives many of the same epistemological and theological concerns that Hodge struggled with so publicly. Hodge's challenge to Darwinism has to be seen precisely against this background, because Darwinism attacked virtually every aspect of Hodge's Princeton paradigm. And the same (almost) direct line could be drawn from the kind of challenge that Darwinism represented to Hodge's world view, right through to contemporary neo-Darwinian and evolutionary epistemological challenges to theology today.

Any attempt to understand Hodge as a theologian of his own culture must carefully consider Hodge's well-known arguments against Darwinism. The British historian of science John Brooke has argued how important it is to note that Hodge's writings on Darwin never took on the character of a diatribe against Darwin himself. In fact, Hodge himself apparently saw no reason in scripture to reject the 'science' behind the theory of evolution out of hand. Hodge, therefore, was clearly no biblicist in the usual sense of the word (cf. Brooke 1991: 303f., also Gundlach 1995: 105–49). He also had no intrinsic objection to the idea of theistic evolution where the development of new species would be under divine control. For Charles Hodge Mr Darwin could therefore be right in his science, but very wrong in his philosophy. This did afford a certain openness towards Charles Darwin, which clearly resulted in Hodge being very fair to Darwin. This was most clearly illustrated in Hodge's well-known statement that neither the 'theory of evolution', nor 'Mr Darwin himself' should necessarily be seen as atheistic in the sense that an original creator was denied. Darwinism, however, as a process in which natural selection worked on random variations, was effectively atheistic because of the complete loss of divine providence and of design. For Hodge this would always be the crucial point in his ongoing critique of Darwinism.

So, the assertion of incompatibility between Darwinism and a Christian world view hinged on the antithesis between chance and design: a point that Hodge understood so much better than later fundamentalists and creationists. And even if it were easy today to relegate Hodge to a rather distant intellectual past, a careful analysis of the evolution of the history of ideas that shaped the history of the 'theology and science debate' during the past one hundred years clearly shows that Hodge here correctly sensed what would follow: Darwinism could indeed be inflated (as could natural science itself) to such a complete and comprehensive, naturalistic world view that it could become a rival, or even a counter-religion (cf. Brooke 1991: 305). As we will see later, this is precisely still the point today in the ongoing debate between contemporary theologians and passionate neo-Darwinists like Richard Dawkins.

Within this context it is clear that Hodge, especially in *What is Darwinism?*, carefully qualified his stance regarding the evolutionary theory of natural selection: he did not dismiss Darwin's reputation as a scientist/naturalist, and he did not – contrary to what could be expected from him as a dogmatic theologian – place Darwinism in direct conflict with either the authority of scripture or with the doctrine of creation as such. Instead, Hodge had framed the question of Darwinism v. Design mostly in terms of the Christian doctrine of providence, and he in fact left open the possibility of an alternative interpretation of the Darwinian thesis which might actually still include divine involvement (cf. Burnett 1994: 29).

This again reveals the ease with which Hodge moved to

and fro between theology and the science of his day, and it says a lot about his assumptions about scientific rationality within the context of the intellectual culture of this time. Science, of course, was not even remotely as specialized as it would become later, and it was generally accepted that educated non-specialists could be part of the ongoing conversation. More important, though, is Hodge's assumption that theology stands in an unbroken relationship with the other sciences: even if their methodologies differed greatly, they both dealt with their own kinds of facts and therefore expressed a fundamental epistemological commensurability. In this sense theology and science, both in their different ways, were seen to share a unified standard of human rationality (Burnett 1994: 31). As such this position was already remarkable, since Hodge apparently did not feel himself, or his theology, caught up yet in the kind of modernist dilemma where scientific rationality reigned supreme and religious/theological reflection was relegated to the level of mere subjective opinion. Even if we were to agree that Hodge's philosophical-theological views today represent an extinct position in the history of theological ideas in North America, we would still have to acknowledge that Hodge's position certainly anticipated much of the contemporary postfoundationalist quests for a more comprehensive vision of human rationality.

This also explains why Hodge felt the need to come back to Darwin's views in *What is Darwinism?* In Hodge's opinion Darwinism had become a 'theory of the universe' (cf. Hodge 1994: 64), or in today's jargon, almost a theory of everything, a cosmological theory that has grown to a full-scale alternative to any design-oriented theology of nature (cf. Burnett 1994: 32). At the same time Charles Hodge was very much aware of the fact that the definition of 'science' was for ever changing: what now were included under 'science' were only the natural sciences, with the specific exclusion of ethics and religion (cf. Hodge 1994: 127). Hodge was in fact witnessing the beginnings of an epistemological development what would affect the theology and science dialogue for the next hundred years: first the challenge of positivism and modernist foundationalism, with the inevitable marginalization of religion and theology, then the fragmentation and pluralism of nonfoundationalist postmodernism.

So, in spite of Hodge's extinct theological position and its related espistemological foundationalism, the interdisciplinary philosophical issues that were at stake at the time seem to have been addressed with a rather robust choice for the 'Princeton paradigm' as, in the eyes of Hodge and his close colleagues, the most viable model of rationality of the day. As we saw earlier, Hodge's discussion of these interdisciplinary issues is of direct importance for us today: although an historically extinct position, both theologically and philosophically, the same issues are alive and well in our times. Not only the problem of scientific rationality, and whether and how it relates to theological rationality, but especially the problem of design – and with it the possibility of a teleological explanation in the sciences – are today raised anew by leading cosmologists (Stephen Hawking, Frank Tipler, Paul Davies, et al.), neo-Darwinian evolutionary biologists (Richard Dawkins, Stephen Jay Gould, et al), and evolutionary epistemologists like Franz Wuketits.

The 'Princeton paradigm' was Hodge's way of hanging on to a fast-changing world: the generous empiricism of Scottish common sense realism was giving way to more positivistic conceptions of scientific rationality that would ultimately turn out to be even more problematical. In his response to the fast-growing positivist and naturalist notions of science, Hodge did grasp well how science and metascience always go together very closely, and at least in this sense I would argue that Hodge indeed had a strong sense of how the activities of the scientific community defined that community itself, and as such also defined what science should be. Along with this, theology was already being transplanted from a rather privileged setting within the sciences to a more accessory, if not marginalized, status. This is why Hodge so passionately needed the notion of 'design', so that theology and science would not just be superficially harmonized while avoiding any real intellectual contact between them (cf. Burnett 1994: 37). For Hodge the denial of design was tantamount to atheism. But the concept of design never functioned for Hodge as only a platform for an argument for God's existence. It was much rather, as Andrew Burnett has suggested, the controlling metaphor or paradigm of Hodge's whole theology of nature, as well as of his model for a relationship of theology and science (cf. 1994: 38f.). Burnett has also shown convincingly that Hodge's implicit theology of nature should not be limited too narrowly to the scope of either a natural theological argument from design, or a Reformed theological argument to design: Hodge in fact invoked design both as a starting point and as a conclusion in some arguments (cf. Burnett 1994: 40).

Finally, Scottish realism might indeed be the biggest liability in evaluating today Charles Hodge's place in American intellectual history (cf. Kuklick 1997: 10). At least the following could, however, also be said: the Scottish common sense philosophical tradition invoked by Hodge certainly at least provided a broad approach to several of the methodological questions that later in our century would be addressed under the rubric of the philosophy of science (cf. Burnett 1994: 53). Epistemologically Hodge was a realist who believed that human perceptual abilities and belief dispositions were reliable guides to the real world, the things as they were in themselves. Hodge, as a Reformed theologian, was obviously also committed to the idea of the unity of truth. He also, however, was a fallibilist, excluding from the outset any illusion of establishing absolute certainty about the truth of what we believe. Both this fallibilism, however minimalist, and his ambitious interdisciplinary theology of nature, should surely count for something in a pluralist, postmodern culture where even Reformed theology often too easily gives up on its public voice.

Hodge's conviction that Darwinism had become a full-scale 'theory of the universe' was at the heart of his opinion that the theory of evolution by natural selection was now offering a complete alternative vision to any design-oriented theology of nature. Hodge therefore understood very well that the Darwinian challenge to theology was complex and dangerous: Darwin's theory not only showed how effectively nature could counterfeit design, but it was a direct challenge to orthodox views of God. On this point Hodge was quite clear: to take design out of the process would be to take God out of the process, and precisely for that reason Darwinism was regarded by him as atheism. It would be quite easy to show, however, that even if Darwinism challenged orthodox – and most certainly deistic – notions of God, Darwin himself never presumed to explain the ultimate origins of the earth, or even of the first living forms (cf. Brooke 1985: 28). For many early Darwinists, like Asa Gray, natural selection and natural theology could therefore very well co-exist peacefully.

Darwin, however, insisted with good reasons that natural theology's watchmaker God-of-design had been made redundant by his theory. He had, after all, provided an alternative account of how adaptations in nature had come about by gradual refinement over immense periods of time. Darwin's precise achievement was to show how the process of speciation could be understood as a natural process obeying the same kinds of law that operated in any branch of the sciences. Darwin thus effectively knocked down the remote designer God of deism, but also the seriously problematic notion of a God-of-the-gaps, who traditionally survived in the gaps of scientific ignorance, only to be pushed out later as scientific knowledge increased (cf. Brooke 1985: 30). But it would be seriously problematic to say that therefore God and evolution had become mutually exclusive. What Darwin did manage to show, and is still continuing to show us today, is that – at least for some of us who are theologians – traditional images of a totally transcendent God had been seriously overdrawn. As we will see, a theistic notion of God which includes a strong notion of God's immanence and involvement with the world may actually be rendered more plausible by Darwinian evolution. After Darwin it has become impossible for Christian believers to think of God in the semi-deist image of an absentee landlord who only interferes on rare occasions. Darwin, to his credit, sharpened up the choice: it would now be a question of all or nothing. God is either an active participant, immanent in the world, or completely absent (cf. Brooke 1985: 32f.).

Duet or Duel?

Religion as a 'virus of the mind': is evolution the cause or cure?

When we now turn our attention to the one of the most important contemporary appropriations of Darwin's theory of evolution by natural selection, it quickly becomes clear that, like physics, biology too has developed on two levels: on the one hand, and on a macro level, the big-scale history of living species, and on the other hand, stunning developments on the level of the microscopically small. One thing that Darwin did not have was a unit of heredity that would explain what it might mean for living species to inherit traits from their earlier generations. This is the reason why in our century the spectacular development of genetics has so greatly advanced our understanding of the inheritance of variations, a process about which Darwin could only speculate. All of this changed with the so-called 'modern synthesis', when earlier this century evolutionary biology and genetics were brought together in a systematic neo-Darwinian framework (cf. Barbour 1997: 223f.). From now on mutations, and the random recombinations of the units of heredity (genes) from two parents, would unambiguously be seen to be the main sources of all variation. Since Darwin's day, scientists have accumulated an immense amount of evidence supporting both the historical occurrence of evolution and the hypothesis that variations and the process of natural selection are the main causes of evolutionary change. Molecular biology, by discovering DNA, has virtually discovered the 'secret of life' (cf. Rolston1996: 64), and evolutionary history has located the secret of life in natural selection operating over incremental variations across enormous time spans. Holmes Rolston gives a vivid rendition of how the two levels

of biology have now been creatively and theoretically interrelated: the genetic level supplies variations, does the coding
of life, and constructs molecular proteins; organisms then
cope at their native-range levels, inhabiting ecosystems; and
species are selected and transformed as they track changing
environments across deep evolutionary time (cf. 1996: 64).

In stark contrast to what we saw earlier in cosmology,
however, the process of evolution does not seem to be fine-
tuned at all: evolutionary history can really seem random and
makeshift, genetic variations bubble up without regard to the
needs of the organism, and evolutionary selective forces select
for survival without regard to advance or progress at all. For
exactly this reason most evolutionary theorists insist that
nothing in natural selection theory ever guarantees any kind
of progress. And because of this, biologists and zoologists like
Richard Dawkins (in contrast to many cosmologists) are
mostly radically anti-theological. Holmes Rolston, therefore,
seems to be right: outspokenly monotheistic biologists are
as rare as those who think physics is compatible with monotheism are common (cf. 1996: 65). Biologists therefore often
typically insist that in the light of chance and contingency
God is finally and effectively eliminated from our frameworks
of thinking. This stance, of course, goes directly against those
believers who – throughout history – have reflected deeply on
the origins and nature of the universe and who have consistently concluded that the universe is not self-explanatory,
but requires some explanation beyond itself. Over against the
theistic belief in a Creator God who brings the universe into
existence, the second half of this century has indeed given us
a new and self-confident movement which claims that any
theory of creation is unnecessary and that science's superior
way of explaining our world and its origins is in fact incom-

patible with religious faith. This movement is generally called evolutionary naturalism (cf. Ward 1996: 8).

Science in the form of naturalism pretends to claim cool analysis and dispassionate observation (for some atheistic scientists, truth is found only in what can be measured and experimentally tested). Keith Ward goes even further and labels this kind of science scientistic barbarism, which sees the study of the humanities, of literature, philosophy, history and art, as useless time-wasting (cf. 1996: 10). Thanks to the radical contextualization and localization of postmodern science, many of us are ready to accept that science is, of course, never so 'objective' and dispassionate at all, and that even the scientific attitude itself is deeply imbued with personal and communal values. A postfoundationalist view of the radical limitations of scientific rationality has also taught us that not only should the truly scientific mind be open to forms of truth which lie in the area of personal life and relationships, but that all our knowledge – including our manicured scientific knowledge – can in fact only be approached through personal commitment, strong preferences and deep involvement.

In glaring contrast to nuanced, postfoundationalist views of scientific rationality, some of the most dramatic examples of scientism (cf. Stenmark 1997) are today found in evolutionary world views which are resolutely naturalist and in direct challenges to any reference to an idea of purpose and value in the universe. On this point Keith Ward points to Richard Dawkins, Stephen Hawking, Francis Crick, Carl Sagan, Peter Atkins, et al., who have all published books that openly deride religion and religious beliefs, while claiming the authority of their own scientific work for their attacks on religion. Ward is sharp and to the point: the anti-religious claims of these scientists are seriously misplaced, since their scientific work in fact has no particular relevance to the truth of falsity of most religious claims. Moreover, 'when they do stray into the fields of philosophy, they ignore both the history and the diversity of philosophical viewpoints, pretending that materialist views are almost universally held, when, in fact, they are held only by a fairly small minority among philosophers ("theologian", of course, is for them only a term of abuse)' (cf. Ward 1996: 11). For Ward it also is clear that the attitudes of some of these scientistic naturalists are, ironically, both anti-religious and anti-scientific at the same time, since they do not consider carefully and rigorously the claims of major theologians, but are content to lampoon the crudest versions of the most naive religious doctrines they can find and thus show a contempt for religion which can only be termed prejudice (cf. 1996: 12).

Keith Ward's strong statements will have to be evaluated carefully, and it really seems that Darwin's increasingly dangerous duet with religion is again growing into a full-fledged duel between religion and science today. We are therefore challenged to evaluate carefully some of the most important statements by evolutionary naturalists and then to show that the scientific statements of these radical naturalists do not necessarily carry the implications for religious beliefs that they are claimed to carry. This is especially true for the impressive body of work produced by Richard Dawkins and the resulting, consistent claim that there is a strong conflict between theistic belief and neo-Darwinism. In the final part of this chapter we therefore turn our attention to the work of Richard Dawkins, arguably the most celebrated and articulate neo-Darwinian today.

Richard Dawkins' reputation as a scientist is founded on

his remarkable writing achievement, starting with *The Selfish Gene* (1976), and followed by influential and controversial books like *The Blind Watchmaker* (1986), *River out of Eden* (1995), and *Climbing Mount Improbable* (1996). Right from the start Dawkins challenged one of the most important and popular misconceptions about evolution, i.e., the misconception that evolution works at the level of the group or species and that it somehow has something to do with the balance of nature. Right from the start Dawkins also consistently and relentlessly argued that evolution works at the level of the gene, and as such exemplifies a process of gene survival in which genes would occupy and then discard bodies. In this ongoing process it was obvious that evolution would favour strategies that cause as many of an animal's genes as possible to survive. The survival of genes, and specifically of DNA, can therefore be seen as the true utility function of life. The unfolding of all events in the natural biological world is therefore directed by the slow, gradual process of natural selection, and this process itself is based entirely on the maximization of the survival of DNA.

Dawkins is still most comfortable when dealing with the pure, incontestable logic of Darwinian evolution (cf. Parker 1996: 41f.). This surfaces admirably in his most recent book, *Climbing Mount Improbable* (1996), where he uses a new and fresh metaphor to make the immense gradual process of evolution by natural selection as persuasive and comprehensible as possible. On the peaks of Mount Improbable are found the stunning, complex achievements of the process of evolution, like the spider web, the camouflage of the stick insect, the human eye, and the human brain (cf. Dawkins 1996: 79ff.,138ff.). It would seem that one has to scale sheer cliffs of improbability to reach such complexity by natural selection, but Dawkins points to the incredibly long, winding paths that lead to the summit of Mount Improbable – paths that have the gentlest of slopes and no freakish upward leaps (cf. Parker 1996: 43). And the information for this incredible, unconscious Darwinian fine-tuning is stored genetically in the DNA code and spread over millions of individual bodies, shuttling from body to body via the processes of reproduction. In his own striking words:

> Evolution is an enchanted loom of shuttling DNA codes, whose evanescent patterns, as they dance their partners through geological deep time, weave a massive database of ancestral wisdom, a digitally coded inscription of ancestral worlds and what it took to survive in them. The main lesson is . . . that the evolutionary high ground cannot be approached hastily. Even the most difficult problems can be solved, and even the most precipitous heights can be scaled, if only a slow, gradual, step-by-step pathway can be found (1996: 236).

A crucial feature of the process of evolution is, therefore, its gradualness: evolution must be gradual when it explains the coming into existence of complex objects like the eye, or the human brain. In fact, without this gradualness evolution ceases to have any explanatory power, and we would be back to what Dawkins calls a 'miracle', i.e., the total absence of any explanation (cf. 1995b: 97).

Dawkins' views on the incredible complexity of the on-going, gradual process of evolution by natural selection also frames his views on the role of progress in evolution. Precisely on the important and controversial point of progress in evolution, he has been extremely careful and nuanced. Richard

Dawkins has always strongly opposed mistaken and naive ideas on progress in evolution, especially the idea that all living creatures can be arranged on a ladder, a kind of phylogenetic scale, with humans ultimately at the top of this ladder. Not only should we not treat humans as being on the top, but we should also not see the animal kingdom as being layered, as we so often do. For Dawkins this mistaken view of evolutionary progress is 'just a logical error. Evolution is a branching tree and that's all there is to it' (cf. Miele 1995: 84). As far as evolution within one lineage goes, however, there could very well be progress as we move from the distant past, through more recent descendants, up to the present. Adaptations to the a-biotic environment (like the weather) would represent no progress, since evolutionary change would simply track the weather: if it gets cold, we would grow thick coats; if it gets warm, we would shed our thick coats. As far as adaptations to the biotic environment go, however, Dawkins is quite willing to talk of a 'progressive arms race' where the only 'improvement' over a previous stage in the evolutionary process would be the ability of DNA to survive. In his own words:

> The better a predator gets at running down prey, the more it pays the prey to shift resources into anti-predator adaptations and out of other aspects of life. There are always trade-offs in the economy of life. If the predators are getting really good at their job, it makes sense for the prey to shift resources, into making better legs for running or better sense organs for detecting the predators ... Given the extraordinary elegance and beauty and complexity of the adaptations that we see all around us in living creatures, I think it's ludicrous to deny that those are the

result of progressive evolution. There has been progress (Miele 1995: 84).

In spite of the famous opening line of *The Selfish Gene*, 'intelligent life on a planet comes of age when it first works out the reason for its own existence' (1976: 1), Dawkins has, of course, been extremely reluctant to tie even a limited notion of progress within our own species to some kind of higher 'purpose'. The ability of our species to ask questions of ultimate meaning, such as 'Who am I? Why am I? or, What is the meaning of life?', has of course been celebrated as the mark of difference between us and other species on this planet. For Richard Dawkins, however, they often are a reflection of our obsession with a purpose that does not exist (cf. H.F. van Huyssteen 1997). This is so because *Homo sapiens* indeed is a deeply purpose-ridden species (cf. Dawkins 1995: 122). In a Darwinian world of selfish genes whose only goal is to maximize DNA survival, however, our eyes are finally opened to a world that has no design, no purpose, no evil, no good, and nothing but blind, pitiless indifference. Dawkins' world is thus finally revealed as a gothic, gloomy world: 'This is a world where DNA neither cares not knows. DNA just is. And we dance to its music' (cf. 1995: 155).

The implications of Richard Dawkins' views for the place of our species, and for human intelligence, consciousness, rationality and religion in this world, are of course, mind-blowing. They are also in dramatic contrast to Paul Davies' views, which we discussed in the previous chapter: there we saw that for Davies our species, *Homo sapiens*, carries the spark of rationality that actually provides the key for understanding our universe, and in this sense we are truly meant to be here (cf. Davies 1992: 232). Davies very specifically did not subscribe to any of our conventional religions, but he nevertheless explicitly argued against the fact that this universe, and this world, could be a purposeless accident. And it is precisely at this point that he emphasized mind, or our conscious awareness of the world, not as an incidental quirk of nature, but as a fundamental facet of reality (cf. Davies 1992: 26). This never meant, in any simplistic way, that we humans are the 'purpose' for which the universe exists, but it did mean that we seem to be part of the ongoing process of evolution in a rather basic way.

An interesting way to approach this problem would be to ask of Richard Dawkins what it should tell us that the ongoing, gradual process of evolution moulds not only the bodies, but also the cognitive maps of different species (cf. Miele 1995: 84). Dawkins has been very honest about the phenomenon of human consciousness and sees it as a deep, philosophically mysterious manifestation of brain activity, which in some sense is a product of Darwinian evolution. We do not as yet, however, really have an idea how consciousness evolved or where it fits into a Darwinian view of biology. Dawkins is, of course, very confident that ultimately the problem of human consciousness, traditionally a deeply philosophical problem, will be 'ripe for a take-over by evolutionary biology once we think how to do it' (cf. Miele 1995: 85). Just the mere fact that the cognitive maps and intellectual abilities of our own species, and our propensity for pursuing knowledge, ultimate meaning and maximal rationality, have been so deeply shaped and moulded by the gradual process of evolution, should, however, raise some very serious problems for us: what are the epistemic ramifications of our (intermediate) place in the ongoing evolutionary process? What does this ongoing process imply for our own consciousness and self-awareness, and for the irrepressible shifts in the cognitive maps of our species?

I will argue that the same evolutionary process, which ultimately will yield for us the kind of comprehensive epistemology that has been our almost relentless quest in this book, at this point reveals something of the natural limitations of human rationality. As we will see in the next and final chapter, the biological origins of human consciousness are complex and often unintelligible. As a result, the resources of human rationality are as complex, and are often shaped by a plethora of equally complex epistemic and non-epistemic values. And even if through natural science the cognitive dimension of human rationality is revealed as possibly our best example of rationality at work, it should not be over-extended to explain everything in our world in the name of natural science.

An interesting challenge on this point would be to look at one of Richard Dawkins' own most fascinating examples, the functioning of the cognitive maps of bees in *River out of Eden* (1995), and to see if – by analogy – we could learn something about the human cognitive map, with its propensity for reasoning and for pursuing knowledge. Dawkins discusses the celebrated 'dance language' of honey bees within the context of the difficulties we have in thinking about 'gradual inter-mediaries' in the slow, ongoing process of evolution (cf. Dawkins 1995: 98–107, 116–19). This famous example from the history of evolution was first revealed in Karl von Frisch's classic work: here the end product of the process of evolution (one of the peaks of Mount Improbable, as Dawkins would call it in his later and most recent book) is so complicated, so ingenious, so far removed from anything we would ordinarily expect an insect to do, that it is hard to imagine the inter-mediaries. The facts, however, are as follows. Honeybees tell each other the whereabouts of flowers by means of a carefully coded dance: if the food is close to the hive, they do a 'round dance', which invariably excites other bees and they rush out to search in the vicinity of the hive. Something very remarkable happens, however, when food is discovered farther away from the hive: the bee who discovered the food now performs not a 'round dance', but rather a so-called 'waggle dance', and its form and timing tell the other bees both the compass direction and the distance of the food from the hive. It is important to know that this 'waggle dance' is performed inside the hive, but on the vertical surface of the comb. And because it is dark inside, other bees cannot see it, but the dance is rather felt, and also heard because of rhythmic piping noises. This 'waggle dance' is in the form of a figure eight, with a straight turn in the middle: and it is the direction of this straight turn, in coded form, that tells the other bees the direction of the food. Of great importance is also the fact that this straight turn does not point directly towards the food. The dance is performed on a vertical surface, and this surface therefore seems to function more like a 'map' pinned vertically to the wall. The bees 'read' this map using the sun, or (if the sun is behind clouds) the direction of polarization of light which tells them where the sun is, and an internal clock (cf. Dawkins 1995: 99–101).

Richard Dawkins' suggested explanation for the strange fact that a bee who recently found food would rush round and round in a figure eight whose straight turn points toward food is as intriguing as it is convincing: the 'waggle dance' that a bee does after finding food quite a distance removed from its hive is in fact a ritualized form of the take-off run. For Dawkins it is clear that natural selection would have favoured any tendency to exaggerate or prolong the take-off run to get other bees to follow and also reach the food. The 'waggle dance' is, therefore, possibly a ritually repeated take-off run (cf. Dawkins 1995: 103).

Now, looking at this fascinating example of complex ritual behaviour in the insect world from a human point of view, we are surely warranted in concluding that through a long process of evolution the cognitive maps of bees have enabled these remarkable little creatures not only to find food successfully and to survive, but especially to develop stunningly complex and successful forms of ritualized behaviour that have greatly benefitted the species over long periods of time. But if we now take seriously Darwinian notions of common ancestry over vast periods of evolutionary time, what does this successful form of ritualized behaviour suggest (if only by analogy) about the evolution of our own cognitive maps and the origins of human consciousness? My suggestion is that it might tell us a lot about human rationality and about ritualized human behaviour, especially ritualized behaviour in religion. It at least minimally suggests that the need for religion, and its pervasiveness in all human cultures throughout the ages, as well as the way that religion and religious behaviour have helped our species to cope with our hopes, with our fears, with the all too human limitations of our cognitive abilities, and with the deeply human quest for ultimate meaning, may ultimately – along with our rational abilities – be deeply factored into our species and into the cognitive maps that have enabled us to survive successfully.

Richard Dawkins has been rather ambivalent about religion: on the one hand he has called religion a 'terrific meme' (cf. Miele 1995: 84; meme is a term coined by Dawkins for units of cultural inheritance, analogous to genes, which are acted upon by natural selection). In this sense it would be true to say that religion has been tremendously successful in helping our species cope with the world. At the same time, however, Dawkins' scientism shines through when he declares that since there obviously is no evidence that religion is true, the success of this meme and its particular form of ritualized behaviour does not have to mean that religion is a 'good thing' (cf. Miele 1995: 84). And in spite of the fact that he does not want to base morality on Darwinism and thus use evolution to determine whether something like religion is good or bad, he does turn around and call religion a virus of the mind, which would make believers victims of this disease, and ritualized, religious behaviour nothing less than sick, or pathological, behaviour. This kind of stance obviously reveals a deep anti-religious prejudice, but also a rather narrow perspective of what human rationality (including natural scientific rationality) is really about.

Dawkins' own wonderful example of ritualized behaviour among bees in fact suggests a way out of this reductionist vision so typical of much of evolutionary naturalism. Instead of being a 'mind virus', and in spite of so much that has gone pathologically wrong in the distant and recent history of the religions of our world, could not the ancient rituals and deep commitment exemplified by religious behaviour also minimally (and analogically) point to some sort of 'waggle dance' that complexly and metaphorically indicates ultimate meaning beyond the 'hives' of the cultures where we now find ourselves? If this were to be at least minimally true, it could possibly reveal our own possible intermediate stage as a species, but more certainly the radical limitations of our current cognitive maps as tools for any kind of 'final explanations'. In a sense this would be a call to trust the phylogenetic memory of our species. This does not in the least mean that ritualized religious behaviour, or the mere longevity of religion on this planet, in any sense suggests an explanation for the existence of God. I am only arguing that, at least minimally, it reveals a universalizing trend in our species' ongoing search for ultimate meaning and for the pervasiveness of the human need to be religious in some or other form. It also reveals the philosophical limitations of scientific rationality: contrary to the overt claims of evolutionary naturalism, natural scientific rationality is not superior to other forms of human rationality. And as we will soon see, it also does not have to be in conflict with religious forms of rationality but can actually complement it admirably. Who knows, the duel between religion and science might indeed be changing to a rather harmonious duet!

Richard Dawkins has been very adamant that all our organs, limbs, eyes, brains and minds, and even our fears and hopes, are the tools by which successful DNA sequences lever themselves into the future (cf. 1995: 175). But if we cannot base morality, and our personal choices for what we see as good or bad, only on Darwinism, should it not be possible – in principle at least – to see religion and its ritualized forms of human behaviour as necessary 'tools' for us to cope with our world(s), especially since it is precisely on religion that human hopes and fears have universally focussed? Dawkins' original purpose in introducing the concept of memes was exactly to say that Darwinism does not have to be tied to genes (cf. Miele 1995: 85). He has also stated, however, that it might not be too helpful to apply Darwinian language too widely and that we should move beyond the brutal world of natural selection where 'nature is red in tooth and claw' (cf. Miele 1995: 82). The only way that we could do this culturally would be by coping with our worlds through maximizing our very own cognitive maps and rational abilities. But to declare in advance that this process should exclude religion might reveal a rather strong personal prejudice against one of the most pervasive and enduring forces of human culture.

Postmodern challenges to science have revealed that we need not feel forced any more to choose between scientific beliefs that are 'objectively' and rationally supported by evidence, and myths and religious faith that are supposed to be 'subjective' and irrational. In resolutely sticking to, and prolonging, these stereotypes (cf. 1995: 37), Richard Dawkins has made a massive modernist choice for scientism in which he not only stereotypes the so-called conflict or duel between religion and science, but speaks all too generically about religion as such. In this context the extreme choice for evolutionary naturalism as almost a theory of everything is revealed as not so much a scientific choice at all, but rather as a protective strategy for making a very personal choice for one research tradition in favour of another. Ironically, of course, this is the only way we get to make choices – even in science. But to claim that this choice itself is 'purely scientific' and therefore not deeply personal, evaluative and moral would be seriously to overestimate the nature and scope of natural scientific rationality itself. It would also imply a serious misunderstanding and a reduction of the rich resources of human rationality, and of the broad scope of the cognitive maps we employ to cope with our increasingly complex world.

God, *chance, and necessity: a better proposal?*

Another recent and direct theological response to evolutionary naturalism was the publication of Keith Ward's *God,*

Chance, and Necessity (1996). In this work Ward not only critiques Richard Dawkins for his resolutely reductionist, scientistic rendition of evolutionary naturalism, but essentially argues that a theistic view of evolution may be a more probable and convincing way to look at evolution by natural selection than Dawkins' naturalist and anti-theological point of view.

Ward takes his cue from the fact that Darwin's hypothesis is quite a simple hypothesis: it requires only that slight mutations occur in the replication of genetic codes, and that there is a great number of replicating organisms competing for survival. The theory of natural selection therefore indeed is a simple and an extremely fruitful one. As a scientific theory it need not, in fact, conflict with religious beliefs at all (1996: 62). Ward then proceeds to make an important argument: there should be no greater difficulty in thinking that God brought living forms into being through a gradual process of evolution than in thinking that creation happened all at once. In many ways the evolutionary account is actually more impressive, since the development of complex and integrated forms which can support consciousness and agency out of simple atomic elements suggests an immense and patient wisdom and a purposive guidance underlying the whole process. Ward is also right in arguing that the fact that the whole cosmos has developed from simplicity and unconsciousness to complexity and self-awareness is quite foundational to our view of science: as we saw in the previous chapter, it really is not only biology, but also cosmology, physics and astronomy that presuppose a generally evolutionary account of the cosmos. From this emerges what will be crucial for Ward's final argument against Richard Dawkins: an evolution from a state where no values are apprehended to a state where values can be both created and enjoyed gives an overwhelming impression of some form of purpose or design. For Ward there is thus every reason to think that a scientific evolutionary account and a religious belief in a guiding creative force are not just compatible, but should be mutually reinforcing (cf.1996: 63).

Nevertheless, Darwin's early opponents were right about one thing: at least some interpretations of the hypothesis of natural selection do conflict with the theistic hypothesis on three main counts:

(i) The process of evolution is normally seen as a non-purposive, random but serendipitous accident. One could argue, of course, that God uses natural selection in order to bring about a special set of purposes that could be obtained in no other way – for instance purposes that require a combination of order and openness in the development of the universe. And Ward is right: this then would be an argument between one interpretation of natural selection and one interpretation of religion, not between natural selection and religion as such (1996: 63f.).

(ii) Some interpretations of natural selection see evolution as a ruthless struggle for survival, in which the strong inherit the earth and the weak are exterminated. If this were a complete account, it would clearly conflict with the theistic view that love and humility are among the most important goals of human existence. Ward, therefore, sets out to show that natural selection is not as such committed to this ruthless interpretation and actually accounts quite well for co-operation and altruism, as well (cf. 1996: 64).

(iii) Some interpretations of natural selection see the emergence of mind, value, purpose and creativity as at best a helpful aid or addition in the battle of genes for their own survival. This would clearly constitute a conflict with any religious view that thinks that the existence of conscious beings is the goal of the evolutionary process, whether it is brought about by natural selection or not. Also on this point Ward wants to argue for the special place of human consciousness in the greater scheme of things (cf. 1996: 64).

One of the main points of Keith Ward's book now is to show that the arguments for these three interpretations of natural selection are remarkably weak and do not carry the authority of the scientific theory of natural selection, which, of course, remains a powerful explanation for a wide range of biological phenomena. The thesis of Ward's book is therefore as follows: a theistic interpretation of evolution and of the findings of the natural sciences is by far the most reasonable (*vis-à-vis* Dawkins), and the idea of God (along with the idea of objective purpose and value) can best provide an explanation for why the universe is as it is (cf. Ward 1996: 13f.). This argument naturally conflicts with the neo-Darwinian view that the theory of natural selection accounts for all biological facts and that for this reason any hypothesis postulating a non-materialist influence should logically fall victim to Occam's razor. This claim, however, can only be valid if natural selection accounts for all biological facts. For Ward, however, it is clear that not only are all the biological facts not known, but natural selection cannot even account for all the known facts (cf. H.F. van Huyssteen 1997: 4).

Ward goes on to argue that the emergence of sentient, rational and moral agents from simple unconscious virus-like cells reveals a clearly purposive process:

> Beginning with a state in which no values or worthwhile states are apprehended at all (where there is no conscious-

ness), and proceeding by the operation of highly elegant physical laws, evolution has arrived at a state in which highly structured, self-replicating organisms know, feel and act (1996: 65).

At the heart of Ward's argument, then, we find that, given the hypothesis of God, together with the postulate that God intelligibly desires the existence of intrinsic values and can therefore be expected to realize some of those desires, the existence of a universe like this follows with virtual certainty (cf. 1996: 65). Ward makes this point by also referring to Arthur Peacocke's statements on a 'propensity for increased complexity' (cf. Peacocke 1993: 66ff.) as an argument against the notion that natural selection is a simpler hypothesis that alone and by itself accounts for all the facts. For Ward this does not explain the emergence of complex life-forms from simpler, unconscious organisms (cf. 1996: 65ff.). Peacocke's notion of a 'propensity for increased complexity' must imply some inherent weighting of evolutionary change which ultimately favours complexity: something natural selection by itself cannot guarantee. Ward is right, of course: by such a 'propensity' Peacocke only means that there has been over biological evolution as a whole an overall trend towards and an increase in complexity (cf. Peacocke 1993: 67). What this does not mean is that the principle of natural selection makes any one particular evolutionary path much more probable than another. Keith Ward, however, certainly wants to argue that it can suggest that, if all the relevant causal and environmental conditions are right (the 'right' mutations occurring in the 'right' environment), organisms with a certain degree of complexity and organization are likely to be selected. That, in turn, is a necessary condition for the existence of consciousness, which is likely to be selected if it ever occurs (cf. Ward 1996: 68).

Ward is clear that for the theist this would mean that the evolutionary process depends entirely upon the right sort of mutations occurring in the right sort of total environmental conditions. For someone who believes in God, the total causal and environmental conditions of evolution are therefore built in and intended by God as Creator. Theists cannot therefore ever think of a universe that is 'natural' in the sense that it is opposed to a 'supernatural' God and would therefore be totally unaffected by God in any way. However, belief in God certainly does not imply a universe that is constantly being interfered with by a God who keeps breaking the laws of nature. Believers in God, on the contrary, are thinking of a universe that is continually kept in existence by a God whose nature inevitably and continuously affects and guides all the processes within it so that in their own nature they express the divine purpose of creation (cf. Ward 1996: 68).

If we now take the next step in the argument with Ward, and say that in this sense it is only the existence of God that can explain the propensity to complexity and consciousness so clearly present in evolution (cf. 1996: 69), would this be a better and more comprehensive argument over against neo-Darwinism, or would it rather be a plausible redescription of the process of evolution in theological terms (cf. Gregersen 1994: 125f.)? I would certainly opt for the latter, since I do not believe that a theological hypothesis should ever compete directly with a scientific hypothesis. If we take seriously, however, the fact that neo-Darwinism as a position is, in fact, a deeply metaphysical position, then there would be no logical or 'objective' way ever to show why the one view is more 'correct' than the other. But theologians can argue with good reasons for a different point of view, for a consistent, more comprehensive and plausible explanation for a world view that goes beyond biology, and as a world view may be a plausible alternative to evolutionary naturalism. But then the choice is not so much for or against theology, or for or against science, but for one world view instead of another. In this sense it indeed becomes possible to accept the theory of evolution as one of the major insights of modern scientific understanding and as a scientific theory that enriches traditional belief in God considerably. And here Ward is right: the dispute therefore moves from having to choose between religion or science, to how evolution operates, i.e., whether by blind chance or by divine providence (cf. Ward 1996: 13).

Conclusion

Essentially, then, in his conversation with Richard Dawkins, Keith Ward also wants to argue that on the grounds of natural selection alone, there seems to be no reason to expect such a definite propensity towards the development of complexity. Natural selection does not claim that more complex organisms will be favoured; it simply says that in the struggle for survival, there will be some winners and some losers (cf. Ward 1996: 69). But there is no way to tell who the winners (or 'fittest') will be. All the principle of natural selection should really claim is that some mutations do not get eliminated in the struggle for life; it is not entitled to claim that the mutations that survive do so because they have a high survival value. Also consciousness, from a resolutely naturalist perspective, can play no role in the causal process of the natural world, and as such is strictly irrelevant to survival.

Yet consciousness has survived rather well in our world, and it looks as if here too the hypothesis does not account for all the biological facts. Ward thus offers a convincing argument against the reductionist claim that the development of distinctive human characteristics like consciousness, morality, rationality, science, religion and art can all be adequately explained by showing that they were conducive to more efficient domination or reproduction (something that sociobiology has claimed, cf. Ward 1996: 71f.).

I think it is now clear that when the principle of natural selection expands and grows into a naturalistic, evolutionary metaphysics, the trouble is that with the aid of hindsight it would eventually be able to explain absolutely everything. On exactly this point Keith Ward has accused Richard Dawkins of the fallacy of cosmic promiscuity: the belief that over a lifetime of the universe anything is possible, even the very improbable. So, given enough time, everything that can happen, will happen (cf. Ward 1996: 117). This leads one to suspect that it is such a general form of explanation that it could never adequately explain the evolution of conscious, rational beings. Ward even quotes Darwin as saying that natural selection is the main, but not exclusive, explanation for evolution. There should therefore be a place for other forms of explanation, and among these might well be the sort of purposive explanation that a theological redescription of the same facts can provide.

Since the theory of natural selection clearly cannot predict that sentient life-forms will come into existence, but in fact makes their existence highly improbable, though possible, Ward has rightly concluded that it is not a completely adequate explanatory theory. For Ward this means that that the hypothesis of God is, therefore, a much better hypothesis than that of natural selection. I would phrase this differently: instead of a competing hypothesis, this argument for the limitations of scientific rationality leads directly to the redescription that is so typical of theology's more comprehensive, interdisciplinary approach. So, from a theological point of view, the development of sentient life-forms from simple organic molecules is very highly probable, whereas on the natural selection hypothesis such development is very highly improbable. On such a view, God and natural selection would obviously not have to be competing hypotheses, and the continuing causal activity of God seems the best explanation of the progress towards greater consciousness and intentionality, which one sees in the actual course of the evolution of life on earth (cf. Ward 1996: 78). In this sense it becomes possible theologically to think of a more satisfactory notion of creation where God at every moment sustains the universe, so that every moment is a moment of creation. With this theological world view we are able to postulate an ultimate spiritual environment for the complex processes of the physical universe, which will exercise influencing constraints on the way it unfolds its own inherent potentialities. On this more holistic theological picture, suffering and death are inevitable parts of a development that involves improvement through conflict and new generation and finds fragile expression in the ability of our species to believe, to hope, and to love (cf. Gregersen 1994: 142). For *Homo sapiens*, suffering and death are therefore not the predominating features of nature. In Keith Ward's words:

The ultimate evolutionary victory, on the theistic hypothesis, does not go to the most ruthless exterminators and most fecund replicators. It will go to beings who learn to co-operate in creating and contemplating values of many sorts, to care for their environment and shape it to greater perfection. It will go to creatures who can found cultures in which scientific understanding, artistic achievement, and religious celebration of being can flourish (Ward 1996: 88).

In a broader interdisciplinary sense, the theologian can therefore with good reason suggest that the evolutionary process indeed seems to be purposive, at least in the important sense that it is an elegant and efficient law-like system for realizing states of great value (cf. Ward 1996: 93). Natural selection all by itself, as we have seen, does not provide a very good explanation of this fact. It actually makes the whole process highly improbable, is unable to predict what is likely to happen, and gives no reason for expecting any trend towards complexity and consciousness. Natural selection, therefore, is undoubtedly an important part of evolution, but to say that it wholly explains evolution is something that even Darwin himself did not believe (cf. Ward 1996: 93).

Finally, as for belief in God, Ward is certainly right that believers do not infer God as an absentee or deistic 'first cause', nor do they construct God as a mere speculative theory. A life of faith is rather a life of complete trust in the interpreted testimony of one's preferred tradition, of commitment to worship and self-transformation, and of loyalty to the deepest experiences one has had of transcendent reality (cf. 1996: 97). God is a hypothesis only in the sense that, if one commits oneself to a life of faith, this theoretically implies a belief that God exists. For believers in God it also entails that God is the Creator of our universe, and that this universe will have a specific character: it will be intelligible, morally ordered and goal-directed (cf. Ward 1996: 98).

For the Christian believer, the experience of faith profoundly mediates a personal presence. The experience of this presence obviously cannot prove the existence of God as a kind of compelling inference for any neutral observer. This deep personal faith does, however, have far-reaching implications: it places religious belief within a wider set of general beliefs about the natural world, and it shows how it integrates coherently with them (cf. Gregersen 1994: 140ff.). From all of this, then, it flows that natural selection cannot be the sole explanation of evolutionary change. Natural selection certainly is an important factor in evolution; but even if a necessary condition it is still not a sufficient condition for emergent evolution (cf. also Ward 1996: 98). This will have important implications for the way we look at the evolution of our own species and especially at the evolution of our ability to know and to believe. It is therefore to the evolution of human knowledge, and what that may mean for religious faith, that we now turn in the final chapter.

4

From Bitter Duel to Graceful Duet

Postfoundationalism in Theology and Science

It is clear that the challenge of Darwinism to the Christian faith has today acquired an almost dramatic and certainly very comprehensive scope. Gone are the days when we could still naively ponder how and where evolution might challenge the Bible, how the opening chapters of Genesis should be read, and to what extent our theological understanding of creation and the origin of life should shape our interpretations of the latest, spectacular discoveries of science. Not only the direct impact of contemporary cosmological theories for our notions of God and for God's presence in the world, but especially the theory of evolution by natural selection has for ever changed our perceptions of the origins of life, of the ongoing development of life processes, of various and complex cultures, of the way we perceive reality, and of the way we now know our concrete embeddedness in this reality.

However, our perceptions of the arrival of our own species on this planet, of the development of human self-awareness and consciousness, and of the radical way our own ability to know ourselves and our world has been impacted by the theory of evolution by natural selection have recently been revealed as possibly the most exciting and crucial issue currently demanding our attention. The special focus of this last chapter will therefore be on our human ability to know our world and ourselves with self-awareness and critical perception. I believe that not only does human rationality have clear biological roots, but that this fact has enormous implications for those of us who are trying to relate religion, or theology, to science. As we will see, the ongoing process of evolution may ultimately even hold the key for linking our ability for rational knowledge to humankind's endless quest for ultimate meaning. If this turns out to be true, then the theory of evolution by natural selection may actually point to the most important link between religion and knowledge, and thus (ironically?) turn out to hold the key to a comprehensive epistemology that may indeed create a conceptual space for a meaningful duet between these two dominant forces in our culture.

Arthur Peacocke has recently argued that as remarkable and significant as is the emergence of self-conscious persons by natural processes beginning with the original Big Bang from which the universe has expanded over the last twelve to fifteen billion years, this should not obscure another important fact about our own species: ours is a relatively late arrival in the universe, even on a time scale of the history of our earth only. Although modern *Homo sapiens* had humanoid, tool-making ancestors, our species only appeared in its present form some 30,000 years ago. How recent this is can be realized if one takes the age of the earth as two 'days' or 48 'hours' (1 'hour' would equal a 100 million years): *Homo sapiens* then appears only at the last stroke of midnight on the second day (cf. Peacocke 1993: 221). It still is true, however, that the biological-historical evidence shows that human nature has emerged only gradually by a continuous process from other forms of primates, and that there are no sudden breaks of any substantial kind in the sequences noted by palaeontologists and anthropologists.

All of this is not to say that the history of human culture represents simply a smooth rising curve. It seems very likely that there must have been, for example, key turning points or periods in the development of speech and language, of social co-operation, and of rituals for burying the dead, ultimately testifying to a belief in some form of life after death (cf. Peacocke 1993: 222). Also here the evidence points to a creature slowly emerging into awareness, with an increasing capacity for consciousness and the possibility for moral responsibility, but also the yearning and the capacity for religious fulfilment. This fact alone, of course, offers fascinating challenges to traditional Christian theology, since it would now not be possible any more to claim some past period in which humans beings possessed moral perfection in a paradisal situation from which there has only been subsequent decline, or a 'fall' from past perfection. In Arthur Peacocke's striking words: we appear to be rising beasts rather than fallen angels! (cf. 1998: 18).

It is important to note that in his *River out of Eden* Richard Dawkins too has included consciousness and the ability for language as among the thresholds that will be crossed naturally in the general development of life on any planet in the universe. According to Dawkins' view, at the inception of life there were no minds, no creativity, and no intention; there was only chemistry (cf. 1995b: 174). We humans, however, are an extremely important manifestation of life, and Dawkins even calls our ability for conscious awareness an 'elaborate and mysterious crossing of the neuron threshold' (1995: 183). In fact, more than twenty years ago, in *The Selfish Gene*, Dawkins already referred to the remarkable evolution of subjective consciousness as the most profound mystery facing modern biology (1976: 59). To this Keith Ward has replied: it is, in fact, more than that; it is a mystery biology can never solve, because it is not a biological mystery to begin with (cf. Ward 1996: 147).

With human consciousness, radically new elements of our reality, like conscious experiences, have come into existence, and along with thoughts have also come values, purposes and ultimately a propensity for rational knowledge. And it is precisely in an attempt to understand our own ability to cope intelligently with an increasingly intelligible world through knowledge that the impact of the theory of evolution is felt far beyond the boundaries of biology. As we saw earlier, the theory of evolution has already become a comprehensive paradigm through which scientists from various fields approach the world and the universe. To this we can now add the important discipline of evolutionary epistemology. Evolutionary epistemology does not generally claim to be an epistemology in the strict philosophical sense of the word, and it is possibly better described as a very focussed investigation into the consequences that the theory of evolution by natural selection may have for philosophical epistemology, for our theories of knowledge, and for the origin and development of our own cognitive structures, our cognitive maps, and abilities (cf. Hančil 1997: 3).

My claim will be that evolutionary epistemology not only yields the kind of postfoundationalist, comprehensive epistemology that had eluded us in a sceptical postmodernist context, but might actually help us to rediscover the resources of human rationality that are shared deeply by both theology and science. I will argue that our theological reflection is radically shaped not only by its social, historical and cultural context, but is also fundamentally shaped by the biological roots of human rationality. In contemporary evolutionary epistemology, then, we will find surprising, if not startling, attempts to facilitate precisely the challenge of a constructive form of postmodernism: the need for a more comprehensive and integrated approach to the problem of human knowledge.

The basic assumption of evolutionary epistemology is that we humans, like all other living beings, result from evolutionary processes and that, consequently, our mental capacities are constrained by the mechanisms of biological evolution. I will accept, at least in a minimalist sense, that all our knowledge, including our scientific and religious knowledge, is grounded in biological evolution. And if human knowledge results from evolution, then the study of evolution will be of extreme importance for an understanding of the phenomenon of knowledge and, therefore, for epistemology. I will also show why evolutionary epistemology meets the need for facilitating a postfoundationalist notion of rationality that ultimately opens up an interdisciplinary space beyond our traditional disciplinary boundaries. Evolutionary epistemology, rightly understood, will therefore facilitate an interdisciplinary account of all our epistemic activities. In the light of my arguments for this thesis, I will argue that Darwin (and neo-Darwinism) was right in arguing that metaphysical and religious beliefs in humans are also related to evolutionary processes and that, even in the broadest sense of the word, human rationality, therefore, has strong biological roots. I will also argue, however, that although this may explain away deistic notions of God, it does not fully explain religious belief and certainly does not explain away belief in God as such.

Duet or Duel?

Evolutionary epistemology: a serious challenge

In the most minimalist sense evolutionary epistemology refers to an evolutionary theory of cognition and knowledge, and thus to the fact that human knowledge, even in its most sophisticated forms, like scientific knowledge, is a direct result of organic evolution. As we already saw, the basic assumption of evolutionary epistemology is indeed that humans, like other living beings, result from evolutionary processes and that, consequently, their mental capacities are constrained by the mechanisms of biological evolution. Evolutionary epistemology today certainly comes in various shapes and guises and may even currently be regarded as somewhat controversial: some portray it as a biological theory, others focus more on its philosophical implications, others may even see it as a new and comprehensive world view (cf. Wuketits 1990: ix). I accept, in at least the minimalist sense, that a postfoundationalist epistemology will only be understood adequately if we also recognize the implications of the fact that all our knowledge – not only our scientific knowledge, but also our religious knowledge – is grounded in biological evolution.

For Christian theology, of course, it will present a special challenge even to discuss and possibly to accept the biological basis of all our knowledge, and from there to evaluate some of the philosophical – and theological – consequences of an evolutionary theory of knowledge. As far as the many and varied forms of evolutionary epistemology go, however, I am focusing only on the one thesis that they all hold in common, i.e., that human knowledge results from organic evolution and that, therefore, the study of evolution is relevant to an understanding of the phenomenon of human knowledge. The evolutionary epistemologist Franz M. Wuketits has argued that Darwin himself has already offered some of the most convincing evidence that humans stem from the animal kingdom and that even their mental capacities result from organic evolution (cf. 1990: 2ff.). Darwin also already raised the question as to the implications of evolutionary principles for mental phenomena like self-consciousness, language and morality. To say, therefore, that our knowledge is explained by evolutionary principles is not to claim that the theory of evolution is a 'theory of everything' or to fall prey to what Keith Ward has called the fallacy of cosmic promiscuity (cf. Ward 1996: 117). It is, rather, to mean, at least minimally, that our mental capacities have their roots in organic evolution and that it is important to study these roots to learn something about the genesis and development of our ability to know and interrelate with our world. This will reveal to us how our mental capacities are constrained by their own history, but also that the biological theory of evolution does not tell us everything about the way we know the world.

For most people who study the process of evolution it is very clear that our species, *Homo sapiens,* differs from the two or three million species now living, especially in our ability to reflect critically upon ourselves and our present situation, our past, and our future. This is especially true of, and directly impacts on, our ability for language, our religious beliefs and our moral systems. Because of this very specific sense in which the human mind appears to be unique in the animal kingdom, on this planet and possibly even in this universe, it is often seen as a direct result of God's special action in the world: a special act of creation by which we humans were created in the 'image of God'. However, as we saw in the previous chapter, it was Darwin who finally destroyed this comfortable belief in the nineteenth century. It is, of course, very clear that we humans do exhibit some abilities that other living beings do not seem to have: we have invented culture, i.e., arts, literature, moral systems, religions, etc. Are these abilities now to be regarded as not the creation of God, but as abilities that have evolved by means of natural forces only? My argument will be that at precisely this point evolutionary epistemology helps us to get out of the difficult position where we feel forced to have to choose between 'naturalism' and 'supernaturalism' as the only options available to us.

I also believe that the process of evolution itself can be seen as a knowledge process. This would imply that Paul Davies was right all along: our conscious awareness of the world is not at all a meaningless and incidental quirk of nature, but is to be seen, rather, as a fundamental facet of reality (cf. Davies 1992: 26). In this sense our species can certainly be seen as carrying the spark of rationality that provides the key for understanding ourselves, our world and our universe. And Davies is right in seeing even the most basic aspects of human thought as ultimately referring back to observations of the physical world. Even those concepts that are most deeply etched in our psyche – such as 'common sense' and 'human rationality' – are those that are genetically programmed at a very deep level in our brains (cf. 1992: 23). Our mental processes, therefore, have evolved as they have precisely because they reflect something of the nature of the evolution of physical world we inhabit. All of this makes it very hard to accept explanations which would argue that the universe came into existence accidentally and that the human mind is a product of blind chance.

Therefore, as we saw earlier, although evolution can

explain why we have, for instance, developed reflexes to dodge falling rocks, it cannot explain why we can understand the laws which govern falling bodies, why these laws are there, and why we have the ability to discover them mathematically. Our human brains therefore are indeed the product of physical processes, but can never be explained by those processes alone (cf. Davies 1992: 171). The laws of nature, our ability to unlock mathematically the secrets of the deeper regularities they point to, and the ultimate 'why' questions that we ask as a result of all of this point to the deeper mystery of the universe of which we and our rational abilities are an integral part. I have argued elsewhere that the nature of human rationality – in the most general sense of the word – consists of the intelligent pursuit of certain epistemic values, of which coping with our world intelligibly is possibly the most important (cf. J.W. van Huyssteen 1998b). This reveals a close connection between intelligibility (our attempts to understand at the deepest possible level) as the epistemic goal of both theology and science, and human intelligence. Various philosophers have argued that it should not at all surprise us that as human beings we could have acquired intelligence, enabling us to secure information and survive in our world. As Nicholas Rescher has correctly argued, intelligence naturally arises through evolutionary processes because it provides a very effective means of survival. Rationality, in the broadest sense of the word, can therefore be seen as conducive to human survival, and the explanation for our cognitive resources as fundamentally Darwinian (cf. Rescher 1992: 3f.). Rescher's observations here are sharp and to the point: the imperative to understand is something altogether basic for *Homo sapiens*. In fact we cannot function, let alone thrive, without reliable information regarding what goes on about us. Intelligence is therefore our peculiar human instrumentality, a matter of our specific evolutionary heritage (cf. Rescher 1992: 5).

Mikael Stenmark has recently argued that this kind of focus on the problem of rationality reveals how much the way we form and hold on to our beliefs in various areas of our lives actually have in common. We are also challenged, however, to find out exactly what it is that the various intellectual domains of our lives have in common (cf. Stenmark 1995: 3). Even on an everyday, pre-analytic level, our judgments and beliefs are regarded as rational if we can appeal to good reasons for having them, and if we can provide those reasons upon request (cf. H. Brown 1990: 183). In fact, it is in our everyday living that we have most of our beliefs: beliefs about other people, about our relationships with them, and about how to cope with our world. Stenmark correctly argues that on this level, in contrast to the more specialized domains of science and religion, we have no real option whether we participate in it or not.

In this sense our everyday beliefs and the choices we make are also paradigm cases of rationality in action, of how we intelligently cope with our world. In religion, too, believers form beliefs about God, or the divine, in terms of concrete situations, so even our religious convictions typically result from learning to cope with our world through experiences of suffering or joy, meaning or meaninglessness, guilt or liberation (cf. Stenmark 1995: 3f.). In the Christian religion, it is by means of theological reflection that we take up the task of accepting or rejecting beliefs and networks of belief and should ask pointedly whether any beliefs of this sort are rationally acceptable. Finally, science, of course, is often regarded as the paradigm example of human rationality at work, as scientists theoretically form beliefs about how many natural and cultural phenomena in our world interact with one another.

This now implies that the natural-selection paradigm can be generalized (or rather, metaphorized) to include some of our most crucial epistemic activities such as learning, thought, science and even religion. Franz Wuketits explains this very well by saying that any living system is an information-processing system and that evolutionary epistemology regards information processing as a general and typical characteristic of all organic nature. We as humans do indeed exhibit the most sophisticated type of gathering and preserving of information about certain important aspects of reality, and this information processing too can certainly be explained as an evolutionary phenomenon (cf. Wuketits 1990: 4). So, also – if not especially – for theologians the following would be true: if we take evolution seriously, we should take evolutionary epistemology seriously. But this will of course mean that, as far as our cognitive abilities go, we will ultimately be challenged to discern whether the theory of evolution by natural selection is adequate for explaining the religious dimensions of human knowledge and rationality.

Wuketits has been remarkably clear on the point that evolutionary epistemology is not destined, therefore, to destroy religion. Unfortunately, however, even he does not grasp how religion and religious knowledge can and should be integrated into this comprehensive epistemology. Finally Wuketits just avoids this difficult issue, but at the same time correctly states that the main purpose of this kind of (evolutionary) epistemology is still to meet the need for a comprehensive approach to the problem of knowledge that will take us beyond the limitations of traditional disciplinary boundaries. Wuketits thus starts his important argument that evolutionary epistemology, rightly understood, has to lead to and imply an interdisciplinary account of our epistemic activities (cf.1990: 4ff.). In fact, not only philosophy but also theology will benefit greatly by incorporating scientific research regarding ourselves as conscious 'knowing subjects' and our genetic make-up, anatomy and physiological abilities into this comprehensive paradigm. Wuketits also sees evolutionary epistemology as the most consistent form of a naturalized epistemology (cf. 1990: 5; also Quine 1971), precisely because it can explain the origins and evolutionary development of the knowing subject. In this broader sense evolutionary epistemology becomes not just an interesting option for theology, but a necessary one, as it opens up a way for revisioning our study of human knowledge by giving us a fresh epistemological look at interdisciplinary issues.

At this point it is important to realize that two distinct programmes seem to be emerging in contemporary forms of evolutionary epistemology: first, the attempt to account for the cognitive mechanisms in animals and humans by extension of the biological theory of evolution to those structures of living systems that are the biological substrates of cognition, like brains, nervous systems, and sense organs (cf. Wuketits 1990: 5); second, the attempt to explain human culture, including science and religion, in terms of evolution, but then not in a sociobiological sense. Both of these programmes are interrelated, but they help us to make an important distinction between two levels of evolutionary epistemology: that of a natural history or biology of knowledge and that of evolutionary epistemology as a metatheory for explaining the development of ideas, scientific theories, religious views and theological models in terms of evolutionary models. Whether we approach this kind of metatheory from a religious/theistic or from a resolutely naturalistic viewpoint will of course determine whether there will be a legitimate place for religion and theological convictions in this comprehensive epistemology. So, again we see that the choice is never just for science and against religion (or *vice versa*), but for or against certain comprehensive world views from which religion and science will emerge as either locked in a deadly duel or cautiously singing that elusive duet!

Evolution and culture

The starting point of evolutionary epistemology – in both the first and second sense – is the fact of evolution. Thus the central question of epistemology – what is human knowledge and how does it arise? – very specifically becomes subject to evolutionary explanations. Franz Wuketits has correctly called the emergence of evolutionary epistemology a truly Copernican turn in philosophical epistemology (cf. 1990: 6). Wuketits calls his own version of evolutionary epistemology a systems theory of evolution, which argues for the relevance of a theory based on, but also going beyond, Darwin's theory of evolution by natural selection. On this view all living systems, including *Homo sapiens*, emerged by means of natural forces and – as for Richard Dawkins – do not depend on any 'supernatural principles' or on the idea that we might have reason to believe in a world created and organized for 'higher purposes' (cf. 1990: 9). As we will see, however, Wuketits is – epistemologically at least – much more nuanced than Richard Dawkins on what the implications of this may be, although both of them will end up being reductionist when unpacking the implications of the scope of our knowledge of the 'real' world. Wuketits certainly groups together all theist believers indiscriminately as 'creationists' and urges all of us to take evolution seriously without this kind of mythology (cf. 1990: 10).

More importantly, however, Wuketits proceeds to explain that from a traditional, Darwinian point of view, evolution is caused by blind mutations and genetic recombinations, and by natural selection working as a directive force. Like Darwin's original view, this view encompasses gradualism and adaptationism. Most evolutionary epistemologists grew up in this Darwinian tradition, and many of their arguments regarding the evolution of cognition are obviously influenced by this tradition. This is true particularly of adaptationism, which normally is part and parcel of the work of many evolutionary epistemologists (cf. Wuketits 1990: 20). Wuketits, however, wants to break free from this tradition and is convinced that evolutionary epistemology requires a non-adaptationist view. For this reason he now turns to conceptions that specifically go beyond Darwin. He now wants to argue that, first, evolution is determined not only by external selection but also by intra-organismic constraints upon evolutionary change; and second, the flow of biological information is not unidirectional but bidirectional (cf.1990: 22). Wuketits now unfolds his systems-theoretical approach to evolution, which first of all implies that environmental change by itself does not suffice as an 'evolutionary pressure'. In fact, organic evolution exhibits patterns of its own dynamics that effectively go beyond environmental constraints. It indeed seems plausible that evolution is influenced by structures and functions of the organism itself. In now developing a view that wants to go beyond Darwin's theory, Wuketits argues that the failure of adaptationism is precisely the supposed dichotomy between organism and environment: not only have environmental forces caused adaptations, but adaptability itself is a systems property of organisms. Wuketits thus proposes a flow of cause and effect in two directions and concludes that in the process of evolution by natural selection organism and environment are co-determined (cf. 1990: 23).

It is therefore extremely important to realize that the evolution of life results from internal (intra-organismic) as well as external (environmental) selection. These internal and external forms of selection work together to build the systems conditions of evolutionary change. And in this sense the systems theory of evolution is indeed a revised and extended version of the classical theory of natural selection. The point is that for Wuketits evolution is an 'open process' and that evolution in fact creates its own laws *a posteriori* (cf. 1990: 24). At the biological level the principles of organic evolution apply fully to the human species: humans, like other organisms, result from organic evolution caused by genetic recombination, mutations, environmental selection and intra-organismic (internal) constraints. But the story of our species is, of course, virtually the story of the growth of the human brain: the ascendance of humankind is due to the pre-eminence of the brain and not only to bodily prowess (cf. Wuketits 1990: 27ff.). And, as we have seen, the one thing that makes our species unique in the animal kingdom is our capacity for culture. The crucial question then becomes: can evolution be extended to culture? Can culture be explained in terms of organic evolution?

Wuketits deals with this extremely important issue by arguing in the following way. First he stresses the thesis that human culture relies on specific brain structures and functions: it is a result of the peculiar development of the human brain and can be regarded as the most sophisticated expression of the brain's power. The main problem that now arises, of course, is whether biological explanations of the brain will be enough to explain the particular paths of our cultural evolution. Wuketits wants to show that it is unwarranted to reduce the complex patterns of human culture to the principle of organic evolution alone (cf 1990: 30f.). Cultural evolution indeed exhibits its own characteristics and systems conditions. Certainly the emergence of culture has been propelled by organic forces, but, however crucial, the biological approach will not be sufficient to explain the complex and peculiar paths of cultural evolution. Clearly, the principles of biological evolution cannot therefore be translated directly into explanations for culture, religion, or society. Wuketits then makes the important statement (which I will argue, *vis-à-vis* both Richard Dawkins and Franz Wuketits, is applicable to religion too):

> Actually there is no adequate biological terminology for the rise and fall of ancient Rome, for the outbreak of World War I, and so on. Culture indeed has evolved, but the principles of cultural evolution are not the same principles we know from organic evolution. We can draw analogies between organic and cultural evolution, but analogies do not really explain the relation between these two types of evolution (cf. 1990: 31).

On the one hand, then, organic evolution – particularly the evolution of the human brain – can be seen as the basis of cultural evolution. On the other hand, however, the latter can never be reduced to the former: cultural evolution requires explanations beyond the biological theory of evolution in its strictest sense. Therefore the term 'evolution' applies to both the development of the organic world, from unicellar organisms to humans, and the development of culture. But we must make a distinction between two types of evolutionary development here, and human culture, when explained in evolutionary terms, is not to be reduced to biological entities. Or in Wuketits' words: biology offers the necessary conditions of culture, but it does not offer the sufficient conditions (cf. 1990: 31).

So the starting point for any evolutionary epistemology is the biological theory of evolution. Hence, evolutionary epistemology is a direct consequence of the biological theory of evolution. We now know evolution is a fact species are not immutable but have evolved over millions of years. And like all other species, *Homo sapiens* is the result of long-term evolutionary processes. From this fact of human evolution it inevitably follows that our mental abilities, our cognitive and knowledge capacities, result from evolutionary processes. Cultural evolution, however (including the evolution of ideas, scientific theories, and religious world views), cannot be reduced to organic evolution. The study of human evolution can therefore clarify the preconditions of cultural evolution, but it cannot explain the particular paths a culture will take (cf. also Wuketits 1990: 33).

Rational knowledge and the origins of metaphysical belief

Evolutionary epistemology has always been closely associated with the work of Konrad Lorenz and Jean Piaget, but it is especially though Karl Popper's views that evolutionary epistemology became a metatheory of science (cf. Wuketits

1990: 45ff.). Although we cannot deal with this issue within the limits of this chapter, Popper is especially important because he already noted intrinsic differences between organic evolution and the evolution of ideas and the fact that the growth of all knowledge consists in the creative modification of previous knowledge. Popper's evolutionary epistemology certainly rested on Darwin's theory of evolution by natural selection, but he was also very critical of Darwinism, especially when used as an overall explanation of the mechanisms of evolution (cf. Wuketits 1990: 47).

One of the central claims of evolutionary epistemology can now be restated as follows: not only has evolution produced cognitive phenomena, but evolution itself can be described as a cognition process or, more precisely, a cognition-gaining process. The thesis that evolution is a cognition process obviously implies that knowledge, and the ability for gaining knowledge, is an information-processing process that would increase an organism's fitness. And already at the pre-rational level, information processing is characterized as a cycle of experience and expectation. So, when we come to the uniqueness of human knowledge, this process of knowledge gaining as information processing turns out to be a universal characteristic of all living beings, which means that human rationality too has a biological basis. And precisely because human rationality everywhere shares deeply in this biological basis, human rationality as such reveals a universal intent that links together all our diverse and complex epistemic activities. It is thus that evolutionary epistemology opens our eyes to the kind of comprehensive epistemology that does not have to emerge as a modernist metanarrative for human knowledge, but that most certainly challenges the radical epistemological fragmentation of a deconstructive, sceptical postmodernism. And if our various and diverse cognitive activities are linked together by the evolutionary resources of human rationality, then evolutionary epistemology succeeds in revealing a space for true interdisciplinary reflection, the kind of epistemic context that would be a safe and friendly space for the ongoing conversation between reasoning strategies as diverse as theology and science.

The biological sources of human rationality is enhanced, furthermore, by Franz Wuketits' very helpful distinction between three levels of information processing that we all share as human beings:

(i) the genetic level, which refers to the development (ontogenesis) of living systems. Genetic information can be transmitted from one generation to the next only by inheritance. Wuketits importantly stresses, however, that this kind of information processing is not to be confused with any kind of cognitive structure (cf. 1990: 55);

(ii) the preconscious level, where all animals require an information-processing system like nervous systems;

(iii) the conscious level: as human beings we have the level of rational knowledge that comes with consciousness. At this level we therefore encounter a level of intellectual information processing and self-awareness that represents the particular state of human consciousness (1990: 55).

We thus see a hierarchy of information processing and also a hierarchy of cognition processing in the living world, and human rational knowledge therefore seems to be the most sophisticated type of information processing to which we have access (cf. Wuketits 1990: 55). Wuketits correctly stresses here that information processing, and therefore the gaining of knowledge, is an important biofunction and indeed can be regarded as a characteristic that increases the organism's fitness in a Darwinian sense. It would be hard to imagine Darwin not agreeing to the formula 'without cognition no survival' (cf. 1990: 58). And in the process of the evolution of knowledge, our interpreted experiences and expectations have a central role to play. I have argued elsewhere that we as humans relate to our worlds through interpreted experience only and that our expectations are therefore always based on our interpreted experiences, but that these experiences in turn lead to new expectations (cf. J.W. van Huyssteen 1998b). Evolutionary epistemology helps us to understand this connection as a result of long-term evolutionary processes. Changing experiences will obviously lead to changed expectations, and the cycle of experience and expectation in the individual is thus clearly the result of evolution.

In a broader sense, of course, the members of a population or a species have often managed to have the same experiences again and again. In the long run, these experiences will be genetically stabilized so that any member of the species will be equipped with what we might want to call 'innate expectations', i.e., a 'programme' of expectations based on the accumulation of the experiences of a species. In this sense, again, evolution can indeed be described as a universal learning process or cognition process (cf. Wuketits 1990: 68). The evolution of living systems thus actually implies an overall increase in cognitive abilities. In Wuketits' words:

Thus we may argue, their evolutionary history has prepared animals to grasp at least some important aspects of the world – those aspects of the world that have been experienced by thousands of individuals during a long line of evolutionary processes (1990: 68).

This process, also called phylogenetical memorizing, explains why kittens snarl at dogs, why many of us almost irrationally fear snakes, etc. And although genetic information itself does not have the character of cognitive structures, such structures certainly can be transmitted genetically. An organism gathers experience through its sense organs and processes this experience through the nervous system. The development of these sense organs and the nervous system in an individual animal depend on specific genetical coding, and in this sense the peculiarity of experiencing aspects of the world is indeed genetically programmed (cf. Wuketits 1990: 68f.). In the light of our earlier discussion of the 'universal traits' of human rationality, and of its biological origin, we can now say that evolutionary epistemology helps us to grasp the fact that processing information is a peculiar trait of any living system and that this trait, like other characteristics, has been developed and stabilized by biological evolution. And as evolution has provided animals with sense organs and nervous mechanisms of ever greater complexity, it reveals a process by which cognition functions for survival and increases an organism's fitness (cf. Wuketits 1990: 69).

Evolutionary epistemology thus reveals the process of evolution as a belief-gaining process, a process that in humans, too, is shaped pre-consciously. All our beliefs, and I would argue, also our religious beliefs, thus have evolutionary origins and were established by mechanisms working reliably in the world of our ancestors. This still does not mean, however, that the theory of evolution by natural selection can offer an adequate explanation for beliefs that far transcend their biological origins. But this does again underline the fact that cognition is a general characteristic of all living beings, and that human rationality, therefore, can only be fully understood if its biological roots are understood. This is true even if human rationality at some important point transcends these biological roots. Precisely this important point has also been argued by Henry Plotkin, who has shown that there is a clear evolutionary link between evolution on a genetic level and the evolution of our intellectual and rational capacities: a relationship, however, that can never be seen to be deterministic in any reductionist sense of the word (cf. 1993: 176ff.). Our rational capacities are thus part of the process of evolution by natural selection, but cannot be understood deterministically. In Plotkin's work this has led to the bold suggestion that the evolution of human rationality becomes comprehensible only if on this level we reject the deterministic influence of genes (cf. Hančil 1997: 17).

Implicit in the evolutionary explanation of the origins of human rationality is also evolutionary epistemology's crucial contribution to contemporary postfoundationalist epistemology: evolutionary epistemology breaks through the traditional modernist subject-object polarization and reveals the basis for a postfoundationalist epistemology by showing, first, that all cognition is a function of active systems that relationally interact with their environments; second, that cognitive capacities are the result of these interactions between organisms and their environments, and these interactions have a long evolutionary history; and third, that cognition is a process that is not to be described as an endless, accumulative chain of adaptations building on one certain foundation, but rather as a complex interactive process in which we move beyond our biological roots without ever losing touch with them (cf. also Wuketits 1990: 96). It is therefore clear that human knowledge is indeed constrained by biological factors, but that it also very much depends on cultural determinants. Precisely in an interaction-ist epistemology the cultural and biological determinants of knowledge would therefore be directly interrelated. Precisely for this reason our rational knowledge also goes beyond what is genetically fixed.

Our ongoing focus here on human rationality helps us to realize that the acquisition of rational knowledge is the latest achievement in the long chain of the evolution of information processing: it can in fact be seen as an amazing evolutionary novelty. Wuketits sees the emergence of human rationality as such an epoch-making event that it has given evolution a new direction (cf. 1990: 108). Unfortunately this leads him to a direct, and rather naive, mistaken perception: because of their rationality, humans are normally said to be unique among all living organisms. But many of those who would basically agree with evolution sometimes apparently hold that humans are an exception because they see rationality as 'God's work' (cf. 1990: 108). In direct opposition to this so-called 'supernaturalist' view, Wuketits argues that from the point of view of evolutionary theory there really is nothing suprarational about our species, although our unique status in nature certainly is uncontestable. Thus Wuketits wants to explain the emergence of life on earth, and of human con-sciousness and rationality, without resorting to any super-natural or 'mystical factor' (1990: 108), and God, supra-naturalism and mysticism are all indescriminatingly lumped together.

Wuketits' basic argument, however, that human rationality and its emergence might be ascribed to a principle of integra-tion and self-organization, i.e., a self-organizing brain pro-viding for ever more and increasingly complex properties, does not have to be in conflict with religion, and with faith in

God at all. Wuketits is certainly right: if self-organization can be regarded as one of the most important characteristics of our universe, then human rationality may also be traced back to the formation or self-organization of brain mechanisms (cf. 1990: 109). His main point therefore is that the brain alone is responsible even for the most sophisticated mental phenomena and that these phenomena are to be explained as particular expressions or properties of the brain. From an evolutionary point of view, then, the human brain is an information-processing system that has increased fitness in the human race, since – as we saw earlier – information processing generally has a certain survival value for any organism.

But what does evolutionary epistemology tell us about the origins of metaphysical and religious beliefs? In order to make his naturalist point consistently, Wuketits now refers to the burial practices of Neanderthals and other early representatives of the species *Homo sapiens*. Obviously these early humans were in need of metaphysical belief, which is clearly documented by their skull cult (cf. 1990: 117). Some kind of metaphysics, therefore, seems to be a general characteristic of all humans. In all human societies we find metaphysical systems which include notions of life after death, the 'other' world, etc. As to how this is to be explained, Wuketits gives a clear – and what he thinks might be an annoying – answer: metaphysical belief is to be explained as a result of particular interactions between early humans and their external world and thus results from specific life conditions (cf. Wuketits 1990: 118). My question, however, would now be the following: why should we, so suddenly and only at this point – the development of this metaphysical aspect of our cultural evolution – so completely distrust the phylogenetic memory of our own ancestors? As with Dawkins, Wuketits' naturalism here reveals a reductionist prejudice against religion, as well as a very reductionist view of religious faith itself.

This prejudice is clearly revealed when not only a reductionist view of religion, but also an inadequate and scientistic view of human rationality, suddenly surfaces: metaphysics is now defined by Wuketits as the human need for metaphysical beliefs, including religion and all other irrational world views (cf. 1990: 118). This superficial treatment of religion is skimmed over by remarking that human beings, as rational beings, are obviously also capable of irrationality: ever since the emergence of rationality humans then have invented irrational belief systems whenever they lacked 'rational' explanations and then went on to project them on to their worlds. Wuketits rather blindly follows the Schopenhauerian idea of anthropomorphic projection here: humans cannot imagine that there might be processes in the universe without any purpose, so they invented the purposeful universe according to their own teleological actions. What Wuketits really wants to do is to explain away all religion by seeing all metaphysics as constrained by emotions and illusions reaching back to the living conditions of prehistoric humankind (cf. 1990: 118).

If metaphysical beliefs, on this naturalistic view at least, do not tell us anything about 'first causes' or 'last purposes' (God), but rather about our own propensity for such beliefs (cf. Wuketits 1990: 118), why then did these evolve on such a massive scale in the history of our species? And why should we distrust our phylogenetic memories only on this point? Obviously, my arguments here should not at all be seen as an attempt at reconstructing an argument for the existence of God, but only for making a case for the meaningfulness and necessity of metaphysical/religious belief, which cannot just be explained away rather naively by seeing it as 'invented' by our sometimes irrational species. I would much rather argue that Darwin (1871) was right in his thesis that metaphysical and religious beliefs in humans were related to evolutionary processes, and that they therefore could be explained like any other mental capacity in the light of human evolution. But this would only make invalid, or explain away, the deistic God of nineteenth-century English natural theology – not theistic belief as such, and certainly not religion. Wuketits is right: our 'marvellous brain' has indeed given rise to creative imagination (cf. 1990: 119), but why would not his earlier relational, or interactionist, epistemological view (his 'systems approach' that even included a weak form of hypothetical realism, cf. 1990: 73ff.) now again be plausible in at least explaining the existence of religion(s) too? Wuketits finally has no 'rational' reason for explaining away religion as 'irrational', nor Richard Dawkins. A resolute naturalism, thinly disguising his positivistic view of natural scientific rationality, not only seems to be inconsistent with his argument that biology can never fully explain culture, but also blinds him to what may lie beyond a strictly scientific rationality and may be only tentatively caught through imagination and religious faith.

So if experience, and the experience of living, is the basis of all our knowledge, then why should only our species' sensory knowledge and its knowledge by scientific inference suddenly be 'rational', and religious knowledge be isolated as knowledge gained by 'mere belief', and therefore irrational (cf. Wuketits 1990: 121)? Amazingly this point of view is actually supported by Wuketits' next argument: if we should ask, 'Are we justified in speaking of cultural evolution like we do of biological evolution?', the answer should be 'yes'. We are not only justified in doing this, but it is necessary, since there is one common trait here: both organic and cultural evolution can be regarded as complex learning processes. Culture can therefore be understood as the most sophisticated learning process, requiring particular modes of explanation and a particular type of evolutionary epistemology that goes beyond strict Darwinism. Wuketits therefore correctly argues that although there are biological constraints upon cultural evolution, culture is not reducible to biological entities. Cultural evolution therefore depends upon specific biological processes, and our cultures therefore are part of a grandiose universal natural history, but cultural evolution, once it started, obeyed its own principles and gave human evolution an entirely new direction, even acting back upon organic evolution (cf. Wuketits 1990: 130f.). Wuketits' own arguments here strongly support the fact that it would be a serious fallacy to use the principles of biological evolution to explain cultural evolution, let alone religious evolution.

Certainly the necessary condition for the emergence of cultural evolution was biological evolution, and particularly the evolution of the human brain. And cultural evolution has channelled the creative human brain: exactly on this point Wuketits himself has argued that, although the human brain is the producer of all culture, this does not mean that the particular pathways of cultural evolution are prescribed by any single brain mechanism. Hence, cultural evolution has its own dynamics, going beyond the dynamics of biological, organic change. Exactly on this point evolutionary epistemology differs seriously from the genetic determinism of sociobiology. But for evolutionary epistemology to be truly nonreductionistic and nondeterministic, we should take seriously the argument that we humans are in a sense genetically disposed to religious and metaphysical beliefs (cf. Wuketits 1990: 155,199).

Holmes Rolston too has argued this point very clearly: in nature information travels intergenerationally through genes, while in culture information travels neurally, as people are educated into transmissible cultures. In nature, the coping skills are coded on chromosomes. In culture, the skills are coded in craftsmen's traditions, in technology manuals, or in religious rituals, texts, and traditions (cf. Rolston 1996: 69). This information transfer on a cultural level can be several orders of magnitude faster than on a genetic level, and can in fact leap over genetic lines. As human beings we have developed a great diversity of cultures, and each heritage is historically conditioned, perpetuated by language, and conventionally established precisely by using symbols with locally effective meanings. Therefore, while animals adapt to their niches, human beings adapt their ecosystems to their needs. For this reason animal and plant behaviour are never determined by anthropological, political, technological, scientific, ethical or religious factors: natural selection pressures are finally relaxed in culture (cf. Rolston 1996: 69). From this it naturally follows that two of our most enduring, most meaningful, and most dominant significant cultural achievements, science and religion, are both products of this remarkable historical development, so intimately entwined with the process of biological evolution, although ultimately not determined by it. Both science and religion not only seek to explain the historically developing worlds they study, but each is itself caught up in this history, each needs to explain itself and the other as part of the amazing cognitive story of our species on earth.

Conclusion

The simple message of evolutionary epistemology thus is that the information that living organisms get from the world is sufficiently accurate to allow for survival and reproduction. The world in which we live indeed seems to be intelligible, at least to some extent, and the structures of this world do not seem to exist only in our imaginations. As epistemological fallibilists we also know, however, that even in science it is never possible to arrive at a complete and definitive understanding of reality. But precisely the epistemological ramifications of the process of evolution allow us to hypothesize about the reality of our world. In this sense most evolutionary epistemologists would claim that the ability to arrive at a relatively accurate understanding of our world is in a sense the ultimate survival value (cf. Hančil 1997: 21). Human rationality, when defined as our ongoing quest for the deepest and most accurate level of understanding (cf. J. W. van Huyssteen 1998b), thus emerges from the heart of the process of evolution by natural selection.

A theological redescription of the ramifications of evolutionary epistemology for human rationality and culture will at this point clearly reveal the possibility of exciting links between theology and science: if our genes do not completely determine our culture and our rational abilities, then it might be as reasonable to expect that our genes, our cultures, and our rational abilities may also not completely determine the enduring and pervasive need of humans for metaphysics and, ultimately, for life-transforming religious faith. This certainly is no argument for the existence of God, but it is an argument for the rationality of religious belief in terms of a non-deterministic theory of evolution by natural selection.

The Christian believer, therefore, is warranted to see the whole history of evolution as superbly well designed to lead to the existence of human consciousness. Or as Keith Ward would put it: it is designed to lead to levels of explanation and reality beyond itself (cf. 1996: 148). For the believer, faith in God is therefore an entirely natural and unforced belief for human beings. Thanks to the profoundly postfoundationalist argument of evolutionary epistemology, we are now able to move beyond the point where our only option is a forced choice between resolute naturalism or radical supernaturalism. Belief in God should be an immediate and natural interpretation of our experience, communicating an underlying personal reality which is like us in some very fundamental aspects (cf. Ward 1996: 153). In Keith Ward's striking words:

> If the goal of the cosmos is to generate consciousness, and if its creator is the supremely conscious agency of God, then the realization of this goal must include a knowledge of the existence of God, of the dependence of the cosmos on God, and of the likeness of mental existence to divine existence. In other words, the goal is likely to lie in the realization of a conscious relationship of the cosmos to its creator (Ward 1996: 187).

Only a theology that takes contemporary science completely seriously will have the ability to develop this kind of complementary view (cf. Watts 1998) between theology and science. It is here that the elusive duet between science and religion finally becomes a reality in the interdisciplinary space created by a postfoundationalist evolutionary epistemology. In this duet theology does not succumb to a allegedly superior natural scientific rationality, and it also does not retreat to the esoteric safe haven of a unique religious rationality. In this exciting duet with science, theology retains its intellectual integrity as a discipline precisely by maintaining its uniquely religious viewpoint in interdisciplinary discussion. By doing this, theology maintains what Niels Gregersen has called its semantic surplus (cf. 1994: 126): the theological redescription of the world, therefore, can never be merely a mirroring of the world of science. It is always, rather, a complementary view in which the very special epistemological focus, distinct experiential dimension and heuristic apparatus of theological reflection creatively illuminate not only the world of science, but also the larger world around it. For the Christian believer, God is never deistically hidden behind life-processes, but is, rather, creatively present in these processes because God's creation and sustenance take place within the individual organisms of these processes (cf. Gregersen 1994: 130ff.). This obviously points to important overlaps, but also to important differences between the world views of science and religion. But it is the redescription offered by the theological viewpoint, the introduction of a completely new and more comprehensive world-view by theology, that remains a challenge to all forms of reductionist science. And finally when we have a graceful duet between science and religion, we will know that science can never prove or disprove the existence of God, but that our scientific understanding of the world is indeed capable of both limiting and expanding the world view offered by a theological description.

In these lectures I have argued, by focussing on some of the exciting challenges from contemporary cosmology and evolution, for an interdisciplinary space where theology and science might explore shared concerns and possible epistemological consonances in an ongoing cross-disciplinary conversation. It is this ongoing conversation that might finally emerge as the 'graceful duet' that has eluded us for so long. By rediscovering the biological roots of human rationality and the shared epistemic resources and problem-solving abilities of our various research strategies, we are freed from being the fideistic prisoners of these research traditions – also in theology and science. In our quest for the values that shape rationality in theology and science, a broader and richer notion of human rationality with distinct biological roots, and with distinct cognitive, evaluative and pragmatic resources, was revealed. Whether in faith, religion, theology or the various sciences, we have good reasons for hanging on to certain beliefs, good reasons for making certain judgments and moral choices, and good reasons for acting in certain ways. In theology, as a critical reflection on religion and religious experience, rationality implies the ability to give an account, to provide a rationale, for the way one thinks, chooses, acts, and believes. Here too theory-acceptance has a distinct cognitive dimension. When we asked what – besides belief – is involved in theory-acceptance, however, the pragmatic and evaluative dimensions of theory-acceptance were revealed. But what does this concretely imply for theology? At the very least it implies that the realist intuitions and faith commitments of experienced Christian faith are relevant epistemic issues that deserve to be taken seriously in our interdisciplinary conversation with science.

Finally, in these lectures I have also briefly explored the thesis that postmodernism, as a contemporary cultural phenomenon, has been unable to come to terms with the issue of human rationality in any positive way. As a result, many of the stereotyped ways of relating theology and science through models of conflict, independence, consonance, harmony, or dialogue were revealed as overly simplistic generalizations about the relationship between these two dominant forces in our culture. The challenge so typical of postmodernist pluralism not only implies a heightened awareness of and a historical sensitivity to the shifting boundaries between theology and science, but in fact makes it very difficult even to speak so generally about 'rationality', 'science', 'religion', 'theology', 'God', or 'divine action'. It is therefore now clear that:

(i) 'theology' and 'science' never exist in such a generalized, abstract sense, but always only in quite specific social, historical, and intellectual contexts;

(ii) the rationality of both theology and the sciences is thus situated within the context of living, developing and changing traditions.

Furthermore, the postmodern mood in theology and the sciences confronted us with serious and quite concrete challenges: it challenged the special and superior status of the natural sciences, and it also rejected all forms of epistemological foundationalism that normally would claim to legitimate either scientific or theological knowledge, practices and decisions. Both theology and science were left seriously and equally fragmented by this process. The result of this postmodernist challenge thus initially seemed to be the unavoidable relativism of complete incommensurability and of distinct rationalities between theology and science, a relativism that would be devastating for any form of interdisciplinary reflection.

To find a safe epistemological space for theology and science beyond this postmodernist challenge, I have proposed a positive appropriation of constructive postmodern reflection by identifying how surprising epistemological overlaps are discovered if the theology and science discussion is recast in postfoundationalist terms (cf. J. W. van Huyssteen 1998a; 1998b). In a postfoundationalist Christian theology the focus will always, and first of all, be on a relentless criticism of our uncritically held assumptions. This should allow us to explore freely and critically the experiential and interpretative roots of all our beliefs and to be open to the fact that even in matters of faith, religious commitment and theological reflection we relate to our world only through interpreted experience. Exactly this point was greatly enhanced by our discussion of evolutionary epistemology. The theologian, in his or her redescription of the world, is thus freed to speak and to reflect from within a personal faith commitment and, in cross-disciplinary conversation with the scientist, to discover patterns that might be consonant and complementary with the Christian world view. The persuasiveness of these patterns should be taken up in critical theological reflection, and in this conversation the shaping roles of interpreted experience, and of tradition, should be carefully evaluated as we ask why and how we hold on to our beliefs about God. In genuine interdisciplinary reflection this should be the definitive move beyond the kind of fideism where our own experiences and explanations are never challenged or contested and where the need for transcommunal and inter-subjective conversation is never taken seriously.

The final goal of these lectures, then, was to show how evolutionary epistemology, rightly understood, can yield true interdisciplinary reflection in theology. As theologians we should be able to enter this pluralist, cross-disciplinary conversation with our personal religious convictions intact and at the same time be theoretically empowered to step beyond the limitations and boundaries of our own religious and disciplinary contexts. This epistemological option for theological reflection (as a contextualized form of religious reflection) is a plausible option because, despite widely divergent personal, disciplinary or religious viewpoints, we still share – even in a pluralist, postmodern culture – the rich resources of human rationality. And because of these shared resources of rationality, we also share an epistemological overlap of beliefs and reasoning strategies that finally may provide a safe space or common ground for a cross-disciplinary conversation between theology and other sciences.

This kind of exploration into the interdisciplinary nature of theological reflection should therefore not only facilitate the revisioning of the nature and standards of theological reflection, but also show how firmly religion and religious reflection are embedded in our culture today. And in this sense the attempt to explore a postfoundationalist space for religion and science is in itself already a challenge to rethink carefully 'high' postmodernism's farewell to reason and the overzealous jettisoning of any attempt to find models for a comprehensive approach to human knowledge.

Probing the problem of interdisciplinary reflection in a postfoundationalist mode should therefore lead to the growing awareness that human rationality can never be adequately housed within one specific reasoning strategy only. To recognize that religious reflection shares in the rich resources of human rationality is to open our eyes to the fact that this rationality itself is operative between our different modes of knowledge and therefore links together different disciplines and reasoning strategies. This will not lead us back to modernist notions of universal reason, but will take us beyond relativist, isolated and sectarian notions of rationality. Thus the important issue of relating religion and science through interdisciplinary reflection challenges us to affirm that human rationality, inseparably bound to its biological roots and to human self-awareness, always grows out of social, political and historical contexts, yet always again surfaces in diverse yet overlapping modes of knowledge. The mere awareness of this challenge, of course, already reveals the breakdown of the traditional modernist demarcation between scientific and non-scientific rationality.

The final challenge presented by the topic of these lectures will have to wait for another time and opportunity. This challenge is to locate theological reflection within the broader context of interdisciplinary reflection. If the search for a comprehensive model of human knowledge adequately reveals human rationality as our species' most distinguishing survival strategy, performatively present in all the various domains of our lives, then the seemingly remote epistemologies of our various reasoning strategies are actually integral parts of webs of theories about the world and ourselves. On this view religious and theological reflection can be equal partners in a democratic, interdisciplinary conversation where the voice of authentic religious commitment might actually be heard in a postmodern, pluralist situation. This kind of theological reflection will share in interdisciplinary standards of rationality which, although always socially and contextually shaped, will not be hopelessly culture- and context-bound: even with widely divergent personal, religious or disciplinary viewpoints, we still share in the rich resources of human rationality.

Bibliography

Anderson, Clifford, B. 1995, *Scientific Laws and Divine Agency* (Princeton Theological Seminary, unpublished paper)

Barbour, Ian G. 1989, 'Creation and Cosmology', in Ted Peters (ed.). *Cosmos as Creation*, Nashville: Abingdon Press

— 1990, *Religion in an Age of Science*, San Francisco: Harper and Row and London: SCM Press

— 1997, *Religion and Science,* San Francisco: Harper and Row and London: SCM Press

Bell, Catherine 1996, 'Modernism and Postmodernism in the Study of Religion', *Religious Studies Review* 22/3, 179–89

Berger, Peter L. 1979, *The Heretical Imperative*, New York: Doubleday and London: Collins

Bernstein, Richard J. 1983, *Beyond Objectivism and Relativism*, Oxford: Basil Blackwell

Brooke, John H. 1985, 'The Relations between Darwin's Science and his Religion', in John Durant (ed.), *Darwinism and Divinity*, Oxford: Basil Blackwell

— 1991, *Science and Religion: Some Historical Perspectives*, Cambridge: Cambridge University Press

Brown, Delwin, 1994, *Boundaries of our Habitations: Tradition and Theological Construction,* New York: SUNY

Brown, Harold 1990, *Rationality*, London and New York: Routledge

Burnett, J. Andrew 1994, *Darwinism and Theologies of Nature: Two 'Old Princetonians' Respond to the Challenge*, Princeton Theological Seminary: unpublished senior thesis

Byrne, James M. 1992, 'Foucault on Continuity: The Postmoderm Challenge to Tradition', *Faith and Philosophy* 9/3

Byrne, James M. 1994, 'Theology and Christian Faith', in Claude Geffré and Werner Jeanrond (eds), *Why Theology?*, *Concilium* 1994/6

Comstock, Gary L. 1989, 'Is Postmodern Religious Dialogue Possible?', *Faith and Philosophy* 6/2

Darwin, Charles 1985, *The Origin of Species*, London: Penguin Books

— 1981, *The Descent of Man*, Princeton: Princeton University Press

Davies, Paul 1983, *God and the New Physics*, New York: Simon and Schuster

— 1992, *The Mind of God. The Scientific Basis for a Rational World*, New York: Simon and Schuster

Dawkins, Richard 1976, *The Selfish Gene*, Oxford: Oxford University Press

— 1986, *The Blind Watchmaker*, New York: W.W. Norton & Co

— 1995, *River out of Eden*, London: Phoenix

— 1996, *Climbing Mount Improbable*, New York: W.W. Norton & Co

Dean, William 1988, *History Making History, The New Historicism in American Religious Thought*, New York: SUNY

Drees, Willem B. 1990, *Beyond the Big Bang. Quantum Cosmologies and God*, La Salle: Open Court

Durant, John (ed.) 1985, *Darwinism and Divinity*, Oxford: Basil Blackwell

Foucault, Michel 1989, *Power/Knowledge: Selected Interviews and Other Writings 1972–1977*, Pantheon Books: New York

Gregersen, Niels H. 1994, 'Theology in a Neo-Darwinian World', in *Studia Theologica: Scandinavian Journal of Theology* 48/2, 125–49

Gregersen, Niels H., and van Huyssteen, J. Wentzel (eds.) 1998, *Rethinking Theology and Science: Six Models for the Current Discussion*, Eerdmans: Grand Rapids

Griffen, David Rae, Beardsley, William A. and Holland, Joe, *Varieties of Postmodern Theology*, SUNY: New York

Gundlach, Bradley J. 1995, *The Evolution Question at Princeton, 1845–1929*. Ph.D Dissertation: University of Rochester,

Bibliography

Rochester, New York

Hančil, Tomáš 1997, 'Evolutionary Epistmology: A Challenge for the Dialogue between Christianity and Evolution', Princeton Theological Seminary: unpublished paper

Harding, Sandra 1996, 'Science is "Good to Think With"', *Social Text*, 46–7, 15–25

Harvey, David 1989, *The Condition of Postmodernity: An Enquiry into the Origins of Cultural Change*, Oxford: Basil Blackwell

Hawking, Stephen 1990, *A Brief History of Time*, New York: Bantam Books

Hodge, Charles 1994, *What is Darwinism?* (ed. Mark A. Noll and David N. Livingston), Grand Rapids: Baker Books

Hodgson, Peter C. 1989, *God in History: Shapes of Freedom*, Nashville: Abingdon

Horgan, John 1996, 'Science Set Free From Truth', *The New York Times*, 16 July 1996

Johnson, George 1996, 'Indian Tribes' Creationists Thwart Archeologists', *The New York Times*, Tuesday, 22 October 1996, C13

Jones, Stanton 1994, 'A Constructive Relationship for Religion with the Science and Profession of Psychology: Perhaps the Boldest Model Yet', *American Psychologist* 49/3

Kitcher, Philip 1993, *The Advancement of Science*, Oxford: Oxford University Press

Knight, Christopher 1995, 'A New Deism? Science, Religion and Revelation', *Modern Believing* 36, October, 38–45

Kuklick, Bruce 1997, 'Charles Hodge, Scottish Realism and the American Philosophical Tradition', paper read at The Hodge Symposium, 22–4 October 1997, Princeton Theological Seminary

Lash, Nicholas, 1985, 'Production and Prospect: Reflections on Christian Hope and Original Sin', in E. McMullin (ed.), *Evolution and Creation*, 273–89, Notre Dame, Indiana: University of Notre Dame Press

Laudan, Larry 1977, *Progress and its Problems: Towards a Theory of Scientific Growth*, London: Routledge and Kegan Paul

Lötter, H.P.P. 1994, 'A Postmodern Philosophy of Science?', *South Africa Journal of Philosophy* 13/3

Lötter, H.P.P. 1995, 'Postmodernism and our Understanding of Science', in *Life in a Postmodern Culture*, ed. G.J. Rossouw, Pretoria: HSRC Press

— 1997, *The Complexity of Science*, Johannesburg: Randse Afrikaanse Universiteit

Lyotard, J.-F. 1984, *The Postmodern Condition: A Report on Knowledge*, Manchester: Manchester University Press

MacIntyre, Alasdair 1988, *Whose Justice? Which Rationality?*, Notre Dame: University of Notre Dame Press

McMullin, Ernan 1981, 'How should Cosmology relate to Theology?', in A.R. Peacocke (ed.), *The Sciences and Theology in the Twentieth Century*

Midgley, Mary 1992, *Science as Salvation. A Modern Myth and its Meaning*, London: Routledge

Miele, Frank 1995, 'Darwin's Dangerous Disciple: An Interview with Richard Dawkins', *Skeptic* 3/4, 80–5

Murphy, Nancey 1990, *Theology in an Age of Scientific Reasoning*, Ithaca: Cornell University Press

Murphy, Nancey and McClendon, James W., 'Distinguishing Modern and Postmodern Theologies', *Modern Theology* 5/3, 199–212

Park, Kevin 1994, *The Mind of God: A Scientific Basis for a Rational World* (unpublished review article, Princeton Theological Seminary)

Parker, Ian 1996, 'Richard Dawkins's Evolution', *The New Yorker*, 9 September, 41–5

Peacocke, Arthur 1993, *Theology for a Scientific Age: Being and Becoming – Natural, Divine, and Human*, London: SCM Press and Minneapolis: Fortress Press

— 1998, 'Welcoming the disguised friend – a positive theological appraisal of biological evolution', in *Evolutionary and Molecular Biology: Scientific Perspectives on Divine Action*, ed. R.J. Russell, F.J. Ayala and W.R. Stoeger, Vatican Observatory and the Center for Theology and the Natural Sciences, Notre Dame, Indiana: University of Notre Dame Press

Percesepe, Gary J. 1991, 'The Unbearable Lightness of Being Postmodern?', *Christian Scholar's Review* 20

Bibliography

Peters, Ted 1989, 'Cosmos as Creation', in Ted Peters (ed.), *Cosmos as Creation*, Nashville: Abingdon Press

Placher, William C. 1989, *Unapologetic Theology: A Christian Voice in a Pluralist Conversation*, Louisville: Westminster/John Knox

Plotkin, Henry 1993, *Darwin Machines and the Nature of Knowledge*, Cambridge: Harvard University Press

Polkinghorne, John 1998, *Belief in God in an Age of Science*, New Haven: Yale University Press

Quine, W.V.O. 1971, *Ontological Relativity and Other Essays*, New York: Columbia University Press

Rescher, Nicholas 1992, *A System of Pragmatic Idealism*, Vol. 1, Princeton: Princeton University Press

Rolston, III, Holmes 1996, 'Science, Religion, and the Future', in *Religion and Science: History, Method, and Dialogue* (ed. W. Mark Richardson and Wesley J. Wildman), London and New York: Routledge

Rossouw, Gedeon J. 1995, 'Theology in a Postmodern Culture: Ten Challenges', in Rossouw, Gedeon J., *Life in a Postmodern Culture*, HSRC Publishers: Pretoria

Rouse, Joseph 1987, *Knowledge and Power: Toward a Political Philosophy of Science*, Ithaca: Cornell University Press

— 1990, 'The Narrative Reconstruction of Science', *Inquiry* 33/2

— 1991a, 'Philosophy of Science and the Persistent Narratives of Modernity', *Studies in History and the Philosophy of Science* 22/1

— 1991b, 'The Politics of Postmodern Philosophy of Science', *Philosophy of Science* 58

Sanders, Andy F. 1991/1992, 'Tacit Knowing – Between Modernism and Postmodernism: A Problem of Coherence', *Tradition and Discovery* XVIII/2

— 1995, 'Traditionalism, Fallibilism and Theological Relativism', *Nederlands Theologisch Tijdschrift* 49/3, 194–214

Schrag, Calvin O. 1989, 'Rationality between Modernity and Postmodernity', in *Life-World and Politics: Between Modernity and Postmodernity*, ed. Stephen K. White, Notre Dame: University of Notre Dame Press

Schrag, Calvin O. 1992, *The Resources of Rationality: A Response to the Postmodern Challenge,* Bloomington/Indianapolis: Indiana University Press

Scott, Janny 1996, 'Postmodern Gravity Deconstructed, Slyly', *The New York Times,* Saturday, 18 May, A1, 22

Sokal, Alan D. 1996, 'Transgressing the Boundaries: Towards a Transformative Hermeneutics of Quantum Gravity', in *Social Text* 46/47, Nos.1 and 2, 217–52

—— 1996, 'A Physicist Experiments with Cultural Studies', *Lingua Franca* 6, No.4, 62–4

Stenmark, Mikael 1995, *Rationality in Science, Religion, and Everyday Life,* Notre Dame: University of Notre Dame Press

—— 1997, 'What is Scientism?', *Religious Studies* 33, 15–33

Stewart, John W. 1995, 'Mediating the Center: Charles Hodge on American Science, Language, Literature, and Politics', *Studies in Reformed Theology and History* 3/1

Stoeger, William R. 1988, 'Contemporary Cosmology and its Implications for the Science-Religion Dialogue', in Robert John Russell, William R. Stoeger SJ, George Koyne SJ (eds.), *Physics, Philosophy, and Theology. A Common Quest for Understanding,* Rome: The Vatican Observatory

Theissen, Gerd 1984 *Biblical Faith,* London: SCM Press

Tilley, Terrence W. (ed.). 1995, *Postmodern Theologies: The Challenge of Religious Diversity,* Orbis Books: New York

Toulmin, Stephen 1985, *The Return to Cosmology: Postmodern Science and the Theology of Nature,* Berkeley: University of California Press

van Huyssteen, Henk F. 1996, *The Mystery at the End of the Universe,* Princeton Theological Seminary (unpublished paper)

—— 1997, *Evolving Towards God,* Princeton Theological Seminary (unpublished paper)

van Huyssteen, J. Wentzel 1989, *Theology and the Justification of Faith: Constructing Theories in Systematic Theology,* Grand Rapids: Eerdmans

—— 1993, 'Critical Realism and God: Can there be Faith after Foundationalism?' in *Intellektueel in Konteks: Opstelle vir Hennie Rossouw,* ed. A.A. van Niekerk, Pretoria: HSRC Publishers

Bibliography

— 1997a, *Essays in Postfoundationalist Theology*, Eerdmans: Grand Rapids

— 1997b, 'Should We Be Trying So Hard To Be Postmodern?' ZYGON: *The Journal of Religion and Science* 32/4, 567–84

— 1998a, *Rethinking Theology and Science: Six Models for the Current Discussion* (edited with Niels Henrik Gregersen), Eerdmans: Grand Rapids

— 1998b, *The Shaping of Rationality in Theology and Science* (forthcoming)

Ward, Keith 1996, *God, Chance and Necessity*, One World: Oxford

Watts, Fraser 1998, 'Science and Theology as Complementary Perspectives', in *Rethinking Theology and Science: Six Models for the Current Discussion*, Grand Rapids: Eerdmans

Worthing, Mark W. 1996, *God, Creation, and Contemporary Physics*, Minneapolis: Fortress Press

Wuketits, Franz M. 1990, *Evolutionary Epistemology; Its Implications for Humankind*, Albany: SUNY Press

Życiński, Joseph M. 1996, 'Metaphysics and Epistemology in Stephen Hawking's Theory of the Creation of the Universe', ZYGON. *Journal of Religion and Science* 31/2, 269–84

— 1997, 'The Laws of Nature and the Immanence of God in the Evolving Universe' (unpublished paper)

Index

Index